T0182547

The Loneliness of the Electric Menorah

Aaron Cometbus

The Loneliness of the Electric Menorah
All contents © 2008 Aaron Cometbus
Copyright renewed 2024
Cover: Bob Brown and Moe
Art: Caroline Paquita
Julia Vinograd's poem is reprinted with permission

ISBN: 979–8–88744–063–7 (paperback)
ISBN: 979–8–88744–072–9 (ebook)
Library of Congress Control Number: 2024930878
Interior design by briandesign

10 9 8 7 6 5 4 3 2 1

PM Press
PO Box 23912
Oakland, CA 94623
www.pmpress.org

Printed in the USA

Thanks to the following people who generously shared
their stories and insights:

Ace Backwords
Alice Schenker
Anna Brown
Anthony Rizzuto
Audrey Goodfriend
Bob Baldock
Bryan Bilby
Bud Plant
Chris King
Don Donahue
Doris Moskowitz
Dorothy Bryant
Eric Yee
Erik Lyngen
Harvey Stafford
Jay Unidos
Jesse Palmer
John Livingston
John Wong
Jon Wobber
Julian Segal

Ken Sarachan
Kent Randolph
Kevin Army
Larry Livermore
Laura Tibbals
Malcolm Margolin
Mark Weiman
Michael Fagan
Pat Cody
Pat Wright
R. Crumb
Robert Eggplant
Robert Eliason
Ron Turner
Sam Bercholz
Sara Olson
Stan Spenger
Tom Alder
plus many others
who prefer to remain
anonymous

Soup
kitchen
↓

(Re)print
mint
↓

shambhala
↓

oe's

Fred Cody
Building
↓

(obscured by
tree)
Cody's
↓

1

Rambam

ONCE UPON A TIME in Berkeley, two incredibly difficult, stubborn men decided to go into business together.

Morris "Moe" Moskowitz later described it as "one of my briefer, poorer partnerships."

Bill Cartwright said, "I'd just as soon not talk about it."

The ill-fated, short-lived venture was on Telegraph Avenue at the corner of Dwight Way. The year was 1963. The place was named after Maimonides, the 12th-century Jewish sage whose work caused so much conflict among different rabbinical sects that Christian authorities were called in to settle the dispute. Predictably, they ordered all his writings burned.

What better namesake for a bookstore? But the acronym for his name in Hebrew had a better ring to it.

Cartwright was driving a cab when they met. Moe was the one with bookstore experience. He had a small shop downtown, but the location was lousy. Cartwright held the lease on that well-trafficked corner near campus, where he planned to open a deli. Instead the two joined forces and Rambam was born.

An ad in the first issue of the *Berkeley Barb* shows

their enthusiasm. "The largest all-paperback bookstore in the world," it brags. "Tomorrow the cosmos!"

In fact, the place was a closet, a fraction of the size of the present storefront, which still manages to feel small. The only things large at Rambam were the egos—and the tempers. Still, the claim wasn't as preposterous as it might sound. The paperback revolution was making good literature and philosophy widely available and affordable for the first time ever, yet only a handful of stores took the trend seriously enough to devote themselves to the cause. San Francisco's City Lights was one, Marty Geisler's Paperbook Gallery in New York another, the latter with a pool out front stocked with live penguins. Closer to home, Berkeley's Cody's Books was also all-paperback. But Cody's sold only new books. Rambam was exclusively—and decidedly—used.

Moe's stormy temperament and his anarchist tendencies are often cited as the reasons he ended up going into business for himself, as if any kind of lasting partnership was impossible. Perhaps. But according to employees who worked for both Moe and Cartwright, their major conflicts were not personal. Foremost, Moe was a natural businessman, while Cartwright was— something else. Moe treated his store as if it was a stage and he was the star of the show. Cartwright acted like it was a prison and he was serving a life sentence. One particular sticking point was Moe's insistence on a generous trade policy, while Cartwright distrusted trade, preferring to deal in cash.

The last straw was rumored to be a dispute about the books themselves. Apparently one owner was taking home way more than the other for his personal collection. Someone cried "thief."

Moe was not a collector or even a voracious reader. Reportedly he kept only one book at home: *The Private Papers of a Bankrupt Bookseller*. I think we can rule him out.

On the other hand, Cartwright liked to talk about sailing, tennis, or places to eat in LA—anything but books. He seemed pained even to discuss the inventory of his own store.

So, who knows?

One thing for sure: Moe was pissed. He'd walked out of his own bar mitzvah—why not this? He came in at night and started packing boxes. Cartwright only discovered the split when he showed up in the morning to open and found half his store gone.

To complicate things further, there was one more partner, a silent one whose role was limited to a capital investment. He was the son of a slaughterhouse rabbi in North Dakota, said to be short and energetic, with good stories and a huge mane of curly, dark hair. His name was Sam Hardin.

Hardin was a public school teacher and a writer, but also something of an inveterate schemer. Malcolm Margolin, publisher of Heyday Books, remembers taking a walk with Hardin through Berkeley. Every third store, whether it sold books or window shades, Hardin had been a partner in.

He just liked to start things, Margolin says. Or maybe he had a short attention span. At the time of their walk, Hardin was running a mailbox rental place on Shattuck Avenue. It lasted a year or two, like everything else.

Anyway, the breakup was an ugly one. The partners had signed a binding contract, and Moe had to fork over a huge sum to buy his way out. Moe paid his former partners off and took the rest of the stock. Cartwright, for his part, kept the lease but promised to stay out of the book business. He planned to open an ice cream parlor instead. Ironically, even in this field Moe had more experience, having run an ice cream stand back in New York.

It just so happened that Cody's Books was vacating their spot right across the street. Though the site was slated to be condemned, Moe rushed over and rented the place.

According to Pat Cody, so anxious was Moe to get out of his partnership with Cartwright, "he had the chutzpah to come over and change the name on our awning while we were still there, three weeks before we left."

"But that was Moe," she added with a sigh.

There are good sighs and bad sighs, so keep in mind that in Pat's 206-page memoir about Cody's Books, Moe—Cody's neighbor for forty years—is not mentioned even once.

As for Cartwright, he broke his promise right away. Borrowing the name from the much-heralded

Paris hangout of Henry Miller and Richard Wright, he opened his own "Shakespeare & Co." bookstore in the old Rambam space.

Cartwright's store was henceforth referred to as "that business over there," says Moe's daughter Doris.

"It took a lot to get Moe to hate somebody," says Bob Baldock. "But when he did, it just didn't go away."

John Wong, another longtime Moe's employee, describes the only time Moe ever set foot in Shakespeare & Co.: "He was chasing a thief. He ran in, realized where he was, and ran right out."

And the thief? Moe left him inside.

2

The Food-Wearing Jew

AUDREY GOODFRIEND IS FAMOUS in activist circles as "the woman who hitchhiked to Canada to meet Emma Goldman but was so nervous she spilled coffee all over Emma's rug." Audrey is understandably miffed about having her life reduced to one small incident that took place when she was eighteen, especially since she's done so much other cool stuff (grew up in a Yiddish-speaking housing project in the Bronx, helped publish a monthly anarchist journal during WWII, made a cross-country Greyhound trip to organize anti-draft anarchists in 1946, started an intentional community on Potrero Hill in 1948—and the list goes on).

Plus, it's embarrassing. The coffee, before it spilled, was the best she'd ever had.

A no less important meeting was one Audrey facilitated. It was at a party in the Castro in 1959. She knew Barb from the Walden School—a Berkeley alternative elementary—where both were founding members. She knew Moe from anarchist circles back east. She introduced the two.

Doris, Barb and Moe's daughter, takes it from there:

"Moe was a failure in his parents' eyes, a complete failure. He's forty years old and evicted. His mother's bailed him out again. He's an artist, a violinist, a painter. He's trying to save the world. And, he just decides to move to California.

"Basically, he came out here and he had an idea. He was at a party, my mother was on a blind date with somebody else, and she really thought he was charming. She thought he was 'crazy like a fox.' And she bankrolled him."

Barb's father had invented the electric heater. There was also some Dupont stock kicking around. In a word, she was rich.

The guy on the blind date will star in my next book. For now, it's mostly Moe.

Barb was part-owner of a Japanese art import store in Berkeley. Moe had framing experience, so they added that angle too. One by one, the other owners were edged out—but business was slow. Moe added a rack of used paperbacks, and that quickly grew. Soon, it took over the store. "Dai-Ichi" was renamed the "Paperback Bookshop" in 1961, though Moe continued to do framing in the back.

The Paperback Bookshop was parlayed into Rambam, as we have seen—the last of several detours on the way to Moe establishing his own store.

With the opening of Moe's Books in 1965, Barb and Moe became—if you'll excuse the expression—a power couple, with Moe out front acting like an ass and Barb somewhere else minding the business aspects and paying the bills.

9

The other power couple on the Ave. were Fred and Pat Cody, who had a similar arrangement. Both women worked from home, where they were also taking care of the kids, as the familiar story goes.

Pat Cody was a writer for *The Economist*. Fred Cody was a WWII pilot from rural West Virginia who'd gone on to study economics at Columbia on the GI Bill. From there he majored in Latin American history in Mexico City and took a PhD in London, writing his thesis on England's role in the Mexican Revolution. ("You'd be surprised!" he said.)

They were intellectuals in the classic sense, including the heavy horn-rimmed glasses—which isn't to say that Barb and Moe weren't. Moe was, after all, a charter member of SDBI, the Society for the Defense of Balding Intellectuals. But they were of a different type.

Fred and Pat had opened their first bookstore on Euclid Avenue on Berkeley's Northside in 1956, then moved across campus to the ground floor of a dump affectionately but not accurately known as the "Telegraph Hilton." Fred called it "the most ramshackle building that ever had the energy to stand."

Now that ramshackle storefront became Moe's, as Cody's moved into their new digs next door.

And so, the Codys and the Moskowitzes became neighbors.

For Cody's the move was long-awaited. Fred and Pat had spent more than a year finding investors, working with architects, and enduring every imaginable construction delay. Their building was brand new but already long overdue. It was a massive structure, grand in design, almost chapel-like, with tall windows flooding the place in natural light. It was beautiful, if that's the kind of thing you like in a bookstore. Formerly the site had been a Shell station, something difficult to imagine on that corner now.

An interesting side note on Cody's design: the building was deliberately set back from the street, making the pavement outside Cody's the only privately owned strip of sidewalk on Telegraph, not subject to laws governing vending or public assembly. The story arose that Cody's had purposely created a "free speech zone," but this is a myth. The truth lies in the city's 1964 plan to make Telegraph a one-way street on the stretch closest to campus. Officially, the reason was to decrease congestion, but the growing street scene was more likely what they hoped to decrease. Businesses on Dwight were torn down in order to create a right-turn lane. A matching left-turn lane was considered for Haste, on the corner where Cody's was being built, so they included a rounded facade and extra sidewalk in the design, just in case.

The reasons for the "free speech zone" were not altruistic ("It wasn't that we were such public-spirited people that we wanted to build a park," Pat said), yet the privately owned sidewalk turned out to be a blessing during later crackdowns on public rallies, concerts, and sidewalk vending. Moe advocated turning the whole street into a pedestrian mall—an idea that's been kicked around ever since (and supported by Amoeba and others) but has never been seriously considered by city hall.

Cody's and Moe's were as different in style and scale as the two men. "Fred was larger than life," says Malcolm Margolin. "He was monumental in his intelligence, in his brilliance. He was passionate in his contempt for people who were doing things cheap and shoddy. His contempt was absolutely biting. When Fred walked into the room, it was magnetic. All the forces of magnetism refocused themselves when he walked in. It was his bigness, his ranginess, his wonderful vitality."

And Moe?

"Moe could have been just as successful opening a chain of muffler shops—and probably just as happy. For Fred and Pat, it was an intellectual endeavor."

Margolin quoted Kierkegaard by way of warning: "Comparison is the root of all unhappiness." Which may be true, but in the case of these two archetypes, it's also impossible to avoid.

A newspaper article from that time describes Moe as "a short, balding man with four cigars and a pencil in his pocket," standing behind the counter of a "musty little shop." Moe himself was even more self-effacing, describing himself as an eclectic failure. "Let's face it, I talk a little loud. I smoke a cigar and my employees ridicule me. Hey, this isn't Waldenbooks."

"The image of the used bookstore owner is a quiet, calm, withdrawn fellow who sits in the corner and drinks coffee and plays chess with friends all day instead of working the store," said Moe. "That's shitass!"

Print Mint founder Alice Schenker says, "Fred thought Moe was a little outrageous, but he put up with him." Margolin describes the relationship as standoffish due to Fred's belief that people stole books from Cody's then sold them at Moe's—a claim Moe hotly denied. Others downplay any sense of rivalry. "They were not antagonistic," says John Wong. "When Cody's had a signing and ran out of books, Fred would call us. Cody's son even worked here for a while checking bags." Wong fondly recalls book scouting with Fred Cody in the South Bay, even though Fred (who collected fiction) found a first edition of *One Hundred Years of Solitude* while Wong (who collects everything) was looking in a different section.

And yet, in the process of writing this piece, only one person—Margolin—spoke fondly of Cody's store. Sentiments ranged from "it was there" to my own feeling that the place kind of sucked and it was a bit of a mystery why it was so celebrated. Without my having to broach the subject, Bob Baldock, longtime Moe's employee, agreed.

"One thing that always burned me was that the legend was always Fred Cody. You know, the ultimate WASP—and what can you say? Here's this slobby, food-wearing, foul-mouthed Jew up against this tall, elegant, Eastern Seaboard WASP puritan. But in fact the real book man there was Moe, even though he didn't much like books. He was the one who had the humanitarian impulse, the quest to learn. Who brought new qualities to the business, the trade. It's not that hard to order new books from a catalog and put them on a shelf and sell them—and, in fact, Fred couldn't even do that. You know, he had to sell the store because he wouldn't allocate. Moe did. Fred wouldn't grant authority to people. He had a young brother (Readers: put quotations around the word when this man uses it) working there named Carl who spoke and wrote about five different languages. Fred would not entrust to him ordering the foreign language books."

Conversely, Moe's talent turned out to be recognizing talent in others. He found hardworking, knowledgeable people, gave them responsibility, and got the hell out of the way. In this manner, he quickly built up a loyal staff that was as innovative and eccentric as he was.

"They were almost like Golden Ghetto characters," Margolin remembers. "Like characters out of Damon Runyan."

Bob Baldock says, "Moe granted autonomy to people who worked for him, if they were workaholics like several of us were, to just really get busy and build a store. He didn't get in your way or have you do things that were less functional than what you could be doing on your own. He was good with that. And so a handful of us built a really good store for him, almost despite himself. Because excellent, out-of-print books meant fundamentally the same to him as dog-eared paperbacks. The assigning of value always sort of perplexed him.

"He got some really good people who really gave a

damn. We had people working in history and foreign languages, and in every department, who had the full scholarly apparatus. And Moe himself did one of two things: he ran downstairs manically shelving used pocketbooks, or he stood at the counter doing shtick."

Moe's own innovation, since the early days of his old downtown store, was a progressive policy on buying and trading in used books. The standard procedure in the used book business was to buy at an absolute minimum and extract the maximum, with no regard to the content of the book, only its condition. Moe set firm rates and posted them above the counter: 30 percent of the cover price in cash, 50 percent in trade. That not only showed respect for return customers, but also for the paperbacks themselves, previously deemed worthless by nearly all dealers.

"The idea was: have quality books, pay fair prices for them, and let it be like a lending library where people come and trade and barter," says Doris Moskowitz. "It was a very good idea, because in a store like this you're dealing with the same people year after year, and they don't want to feel like they're getting burned every time they bring back one of the books they bought from you."

His policy affected the industry as a whole. "Other used book dealers had to contend with this," says Baldock. "It changed the landscape for book lovers." It also meant that, when selling your collection, you went to Moe's first. They picked the best books and paid the highest price. Then you crossed the street to Shakespeare & Co. and they took the rest. (When buying books, you might go in reverse order, since a less picky store often has a more interesting selection.)

One illustrative story about Shakespeare & Co. during this period comes from a book dealer named Ralph. He came in one day when Sam Hardin was manning the counter—an unusual event that only happened when Cartwright was off on one of his rare vacations.

One by one, Hardin carefully looked over Ralph's books, but there seemed to be no rhyme or reason in his process of selection. Finally Ralph realized that Hardin was just picking every other book, but making a show of studying them so as to not seem ignorant.

When Hardin had gone through all the boxes, Ralph had a brainstorm. "You know," he said, "I've got some more books in the car. Let me take these back and I'll bring in some more."

He loaded them onto the hand truck, took them outside, waited a few minutes, then put the same books back on the counter. Hardin selected every other one again.

Ralph did the same thing over and over until he'd nearly gotten rid of them all.

If only we were all so lucky.

Now, before we let the sun set on this particular era of the 2400 block of Telegraph, here's Margolin to describe a typical day at Cody's during Fred's tenure:

"You'd come in at noontime and because of complete misplanning the entire staff had taken off for lunch except for one person at the cash register. The place would be mobbed with students, and everything in complete chaos. And you'd come in, you'd walk to a little room down at the bottom floor. Fred was a tall man, his head would be right up against the ceiling. You'd go through the chaos, people yelling and screaming, and lining up and trying to find things, and kids bawling, and people nodding out. And then you'd open the door, you'd come in, it'd be quiet." Margolin whispers: "And there would be Fred, leaning over a table with a box of books in his hand. 'Malcolm, *look* at this book! Look at what Knopf just did! Look at the binding! Look at the way they designed it! Look at the cover, look at the paper!' Time would just stop. Then we'd go out for coffee and pick our way through the chaos."

Where, I asked Margolin, did they go for coffee?

"A Persian restaurant a block towards campus on the Cody's side," he said. "It was not at the Med."

That was what I wondered, and as I'd suspected. Cody and the Med didn't seem to mix. Margolin agreed: Fred would look out of place. He explained, "What we wanted to do is go out for a cup of coffee and talk. And the Med is such a public marketplace that you couldn't go there without meeting ninety-five unpleasant characters that had some kind of trip that they wanted to lay on you. Or they wanted to tell you the same story that they told you seventeen times before."

This, more than anything else, seems to sum up the difference between the two men. A public market filled with old stories and odd characters was Moe-like in its essence. You could find him there.

If not, Doris or one of Moe's right-hand men would be running over to get him a seltzer and dry cookie or a black coffee. When the Med objected to Moe borrowing their tall glasses, Moe objected back.

3

The Hungry Oy

DON SCHENKER AND MOE were friends from back on the Lower East Side, when Moe's impulsive apartment renovation got him evicted (as ripping out a wall often will) and he became a regular guest at Don and Alice Schenker's place.

Judith Malina met Moe around the same time, remembering him in her memoirs as "one of the anarchists who invaded a Christmas party at my house two years ago carrying a toothbrush in his coat to indicate homelessness." Recognizing a natural-born ham, Malina and Julian Beck cast him as the lead in the Living Theater production of Alfred Jarry's *Ubu Roi*.

She wrote, "Moe Moskowitz, the anarchists' Isis, is our Ubu."

But that's another story.

When Moe headed west, the Schenkers followed and were soon up to their necks in a dubious scheme. As Alice says, "It was impossible to get a good piece of bread or a bagel in San Francisco. There wasn't even a delicatessen of any kind."

So, they set out to create one. A traditional Jewish

deli. A little piece of New York on the Left (or Least) Coast.

Besides the Schenkers and Moe, there was Mike Gries, a *San Francisco Chronicle* reporter, and Mike's cousin, the son of a deli owner back east. This kid knew cold cuts the way country kids knew fields and streams. He was their ringer.

Around the corner from Banducci's famous North Beach nightclub "the Hungry I" was a Chinese pool hall nearing eviction—the perfect spot for their lousy pun. And they were pretty far along with the plan when impossible-to-foresee problems arose. According to Alice, Mike Gries's cousin married an incredibly beautiful Gypsy queen. The Gypsies, never pleased about intermarriage, were particularly unhappy about a Jewish butcher marrying into their royal family. Death threats arrived, followed by a team of assassins ready to carry out the deed. The newlyweds had to drop out of sight, disappearing without a trace.

That was their deli guy, and he was gone. Meanwhile, the Chinese pool players refused to budge. The whole plan just fizzled out, becoming a funny road-not-taken to look back on and wonder "what if?"

Instead, it was then that Moe met Barb and found his future road with her. Don and Alice followed again, this time across the bay. Don set up a framing and mounting workshop called "the Print Mint." Alice worked in a nightclub. By this time, they had two kids.

Don and Moe were the best of friends, and both framers, though this was just a coincidence. They hadn't learned together and never worked together. In fact, it was the only aspect of their lives that didn't overlap. Both thought of framing as an occupation only, secondary to any creative pursuits. For Don that meant writing poetry (a vocation that didn't and doesn't pay) and for Moe—a Cooper Union dropout—painting. (Alice painted too.)

By 1965, the Print Mint was gaining momentum. Alice was able to quit her other job and join Don. Moe invited them to set up a table inside Rambam. From there, they could sell prints of art reproductions and take orders for framing and mounting jobs (the work, then and later, was done off-site). It was a good arrangement, and the old friends were glad to be together again under one roof. However, it lasted only one month before the Big Bang—the explosion between Moe and Cartwright that launched a whole galaxy of quirky stores (though none, it must be said, came from Cartwright's side).

The Schenkers followed Moe across the street, sharing with him the new Telegraph Hilton storefront. Both businesses stretched out, Moe getting more floor space and shelves and Print Mint taking all the walls and even some of the ceiling for their prints, plus a long counter on one side for placing orders. The outside awning was also shared, as can be seen in the movie *The Graduate*, when Dustin Hoffman gazes wistfully across the street from inside the Med.

Then Alice saw a small ad in the back of a magazine for photo posters of actor Jean-Paul Belmondo;

she decided to try those too. Next, some oversize photos of Marlon Brando. Both were immediate hits. Posters had never before been in demand—they were not yet the ubiquitous cultural currency they would soon become.

As demand multiplied, the Schenkers ordered from every obscure source they could find (including the Department of Agriculture for one particularly popular image of eggs). The Print Mint became a poster shop, primarily. Before long they began producing them.

Were they annoyed that their fancy little framing place so quickly morphed into a poster shop? Not at all, says Alice. They were living in the moment and glad to feel a part of changes in the cultural landscape. Besides, the store continued to take framing orders, and one mounting process that Don pioneered was popular and well-suited to their new line: the posters were glued to masonite, the edges beveled, then braced on back; the surface was sprayed with a lacquer that slowed any fading. It was a pleasant and inexpensive alternative to framing—one that became an industry standard, and is still used today.

Just as Print Mint had grown out from under Moe's wings, so did a dozen other businesses in the years to come, many with an expansionist zeal that was frightening. But Moe was not interested in opening satellite versions of Moe's. The sole exception was yet another failed, short-lived project that came to be known as the "Cockamamie Palace."

The idea was for a San Francisco store, this one also shared with the Schenkers, plus space in the basement for a collective that distributed the *Berkeley Barb* and other underground papers. For a location, they chose an out-of-the-way rental area where a lot of SF State students lived. In the mid-'60s, the neighborhood was still sleepy, and the building that Barb Moskowitz bought—a former Woolworth's on Haight near Ashbury—was huge and cheap.

Print Mint moved into the front, and immediately thrived. Their appearance and selection of posters dovetailed perfectly with the first arrival in San Francisco of freaks from around the country—a trickle that soon became a downpour and then the deluge known as the Summer of Love. A September 1967 issue of *Life* magazine had a special report on the emerging scene, with a full-page photo of Print Mint showing the place packed out with curious customers. Lenny Bruce, Mao, Bettie Davis, Einstein, and the Jefferson Airplane look down from oversized posters on the walls. Cheshire Cats, bananas—the whole colorful spectrum of usual and unusual icons.

Print Mint was not the only store selling posters, but one of the few, and posters were just becoming a (counter-) cultural staple. Perhaps books would have become one too, if not for an antiquated San Francisco law requiring a secondhand dealer's license for anyone selling used goods. Moe went to the licensing board for his permit, and was happily surprised when someone on the board recognized him. However, the board member was not a fan. He'd been in the Berkeley store and heard Moe carrying on in all sorts of uncouth ways. He saw in Moe the perfect example of an undesirable— exactly the kind of seedy peddler the board was set up to discourage.

So, every time Moe's permit came up for a vote, it was rejected. Again and again Moe applied. He railed, he stormed, but to no avail—the license would never be granted.

Behind the front section of the Palace, the imaginary demarcation where Print Mint began and Moe's was never to be, lay a huge dead space—and a somewhat dangerous one. As the scene in the Haight degenerated, the Schenkers worried for their employees' safety. A job co-op sometimes used the vacant area, but so did various crashers and thugs. "The Indians took it over for a while," Moe said mysteriously, offering more questions than answers. Drug abuse ruined any hope for the "Third World Distribution" scheme downstairs. Country Joe and the Fish showed up to rehearse—always a sign that the end is near.

It was a total, hopeless mess, and the Schenkers had no means with which to purchase the place for themselves. They were overtaxed anyway, with the Berkeley store and a wholesale business they'd also started, distributing posters. When Barb defaulted on the mortgage, it was a relief for everyone.

"You can't win them all," Moe said.

BERCHOLZ
+FAGAN
IN PARIS

4

The Kingdom of Shambala

SAM BERCHOLZ WAS THE SON of two Polish concentration camp survivors who fell in love in a repatriation center in Sweden. Michael Fagan's family had been in California since 1809. Both worked the graveyard shift at the Rincon Annex post office in downtown San Francisco to pay their way through college.

They unloaded trucks and sorted mail. Then, in the peaceful, blissful emptiness of the true middle of the night, they took breaks and sat talking on the post office steps. It turned out they were both reading the same weird stuff: Madame Blavatsky and Alice Bailey, Gurdjieff and all kinds of theology. They became very close, a kind of "society of one," totally in sync with each other.

Bercholz was only nineteen at the time and already had his own radio show called "Adventures in Consciousness." Fagan was twenty-five. He recalls their late-night conversations reaching a conclusion:

"We thought we should create an energy center, a place where people could come together and explore ideas, discuss, interact. And what would come of it? Let's find out!"

"The simplest way to do this," Fagan says, "was to set up a bookstore."

Berkeley at the time was a mess, "a political polarization process" that didn't interest them at all. San Francisco, on the other hand, was bursting with a sense of enlightenment, "a downpour of energy from the heavens."

However, with all the new arrivals, rents in SF were skyrocketing. Heaven would have to wait. They turned their sights across the bay.

They hit on a bright idea: maybe the guy at Moe's would let them set up their own section. Books on the subjects that interested them—yoga, theology, the occult—which were nearly impossible to find.

"One day we got up the nerve to visit Moe," Bercholz remembers. "We only knew him as the wonderfully eccentric guy that sold us books and played Lenny Bruce and Lord Buckley on his store stereo. I proposed that Moe hire me, and Michael sometime in the future, to set up a special 'comparative religion, mysticism, metaphysical' section in his bookstore. Amazingly, he liked the idea immediately."

Moe had no personal interest whatsoever in religion and the supernatural, but he realized these two kids were bright and their plan was sound. A meeting was set up at the Moskowitz house, where Barb proved enthusiastic as well. Bercholz was hired as the sole employee of a separate entity within Moe's, with an agreement that Fagan would come aboard later once he'd finished school. Barb and Moe retained ownership and put up the money for the books.

Before Cody's and Moe's, the ground floor of the Telegraph Hilton had been a grocery store. A room in the back was where the returned milk and soda bottles were kept. Now a curtain was tacked up and that hole in the wall became what Fagan, in a burst of enthusiasm, called "an oasis on the Avenue."

"This is a test of America," he grandly announced.

Bercholz and Fagan worked around the clock putting bookshelves and insulation into the unfinished, unfurnished room in the back of Moe's. They decorated the place with miniature Buddhas and photos of religious thinkers from around the world. While Bercholz sat in the Med ordering books, Fagan painted signs with cryptic slogans inviting people inside. "Enter the rainbow bridge to Shambala city of the gods," read one. "Welcome to the kingdom of Shambala," said another.

Only one thing missing. Tibetan monk Chögyam Trungpa stopped by and suggested adding an 'h' so that Americans might pronounce the name right.

Very good. And so, Shambhala it was.

Literally, the word in Tibetan means an elevated or happy place. It refers to a mythical city supposed to be the earthly seat of divinity and holiness. Bercholz and Fagan expanded on the definition, using the term to describe any confluence of lofty, high-spirited ideas.

Shambhala opened its curtains in the fall of 1968. The hours were limited to two or three in the afternoon (when Bercholz got out of school and made it over the bridge) until around eight (when he closed up, often headed for a "family" dinner at the Moskowitz home). Its beginnings were humble. "The small room has a warm, intimate atmosphere," wrote a *Daily Californian* reporter. "The people who man the tiny desk are very friendly and seem more interested in talking about books than actually trying to sell them."

But things moved fast. The hours were expanded as two clerks were hired. Fagan graduated college and came to work at the store full-time. Bercholz finished school too, dropping out when the National Guard occupied SF State.

The big change came at the end of the year when Barb Moskowitz bought the building next door—a sprawling giant that took up half the block, including twenty-four apartments and a half-dozen storefronts. Moe's and Print Mint could finally say goodbye to the leaking, creaking Telegraph Hilton. For the first time in their lives, they didn't have to share a room.

But what could Shambhala do? The storefront next to Moe's and Print Mint was already rented to a longtime tenant: the Christian Science Reading Room. They'd been there for fifty years—since Telegraph still had the wires that gave it its name. They weren't going anywhere.

Or were they?

The Reading Room had a lease they assumed would go on in perpetuity. When it lapsed, they didn't bother to renew it until six months later, and by then their option had passed. But why worry? Who on earth would evict a bunch of elderly Christians?

Doris Moskowitz hadn't heard this part of her parents' story, but when I mentioned it, she laughed: "Oh, yeah, that makes sense. I could totally see her doing that."

According to Fagan, the place was just a black hole on the Avenue: "No one went in there, and the books were just collecting dust. So, we moved them out. They were quite upset, but they didn't have anything going, anyway. They could find somewhere else."

"They left the store in mint condition," gloated the new tenants, who had no trouble filling the place with books and customers. "People couldn't wait to get in," Fagan says. "It became a really magnetic situation. And during that time, Telegraph Avenue was okay for most people, so they had no problem about coming down there. Later it got completely taken over by street people and got pretty unsavory." (Only in Berkeley do you find people who nail up "All Hail to the One Cosmic Mind" signs and get Carlos Castaneda to speak in the basement, then complain about unsavory elements arriving in the neighborhood.)

Bercholz and Fagan searched far and wide for esoteric and interesting titles. Other booksellers couldn't be bothered dealing with foreign publishers, often with good reason—Fagan recalls new books arriving from India already worm-infested and covered in mold. Still, Shambhala had tapped into a mostly undiscovered market, and the demand far outstripped the supply. In the process, they made an important discovery: the distribution rights for many hard-to-find titles were readily available. This led to the next unexpected step in their path: publishing.

In 1969, with five hundred dollars each from Bercholz, Fagan, and third partner Phil Wood, Shambhala launched its own imprint with *Meditation in Action* by their old pal Chögyam Trungpa. Other new releases followed, along with reprints of old books whose copyright had expired—the most notorious being Aleister Crowley's on the tarot. Crowley's books were supposedly cursed, and no publisher would touch them. "Heaven would cave in on you if you reprinted them," Fagan says, "God would strike you with a bolt of lightning. But nothing happened except that Crowley's self-styled secretary, who said he owned the rights to everything, tried to get on our case. He said he'd sue us to the end of the earth."

In the end, the "secretary" just made a lot of noise—though he'd successfully intimidated people for years that way. Shambhala was never sued, but the curse took a roundabout route: their fledgling partnership broke up. Phil Wood had to be paid off a huge sum in the quick and unhappy split which seems par for the course for third partners. Wood went on to found Ten Speed Press and strike it rich with mega-selling schlock *What Color is Your Parachute?* (Thirty-five years later, it's still in print.)

Articles on Shambhala's early days all mention a rare unity of purpose among the Telegraph bookstores.

According to the *Berkeley Daily Planet*, "Cody's, Shakespeare & Co., and Moe's agreed not to carry Shambhala's best-selling titles, so that the smaller specialty store would thrive."

Bercholz and Fagan had a field day responding to that claim.

"I don't really think Cody's cared about us," says Bercholz, "other than to have a place to send their customers for what they considered to be strange books."

"Everyone figured out we were successful and tried to get in on the train," Fagan says. "The other bookstores were finding out what was selling and making sure they had more copies than we did."

Everyone but Moe's, who did keep the duplicate titles at a minimum. The fact is, they still owned Shambhala, though it had clearly outgrown their patronage. Payments were spread out over a long period so that Fagan and Bercholz could eventually buy the business.

Bercholz began to spend more and more time in the basement, where Shambhala's publishing wing was located. Fagan managed the store. He says, "It was decided that Sam would go downstairs because he would be a lot more effective that way. It was harder for him to deal with people on an ongoing basis, and we did have some very strange people coming into the store, obviously. He didn't suffer people gladly."

While Bercholz developed contacts in the publishing world and his monster in the basement began to stir (soon to attack as the world's leading producer of freaky New Age crap), yet another business was forming by the front door. Bercholz wanted to create a "buffer from Telegraph Avenue," and the easiest way to do that was to rent the first ten feet of Shambhala to someone else. The opportunity came in 1970 when two employees wanted to open an herb store. Using the original Shambhala-in-Moe's model, a tiny room-within-a-room was cordoned off and sublet. That became Lhasa Karnak.

Lhasa Karnak went on to a long history of its own—the usual bitter partner breakups and eventual expansion; the selling of the business once the founders had burned out.

I tried to interview current Lhasa Karnak owner Jim Murdoch for this piece, but he was a total prick. "I don't care about that stuff," he snapped, nearly yelling at me. "I don't care about the past."

That was fine. Maybe even a refreshing sentiment from someone of a generation so consumed in nostalgia and their own legend. But why be an asshole about it?

Everyone has bad days, but what again was this guy so angry about? It was easy for him to dismiss the past. He owned multiple stores. He had a future, a stage, real estate. For the rest of us, the only thing we'll ever own—especially on the Ave.—is our stories, our collective identity, and our stake in the culture we're part of and trying to maintain. Why make it hard for the rest of us to feel part of that? Why be angry at me for a desire to tie our stories together and share them?

I was livid. If it had been just one Jim Murdoch,

it would have been no problem, but it had been a life-
time of dealing with these smug, self-centered hippie
entrepreneurs—and already three weeks spent kissing
hippie ass in order to write this piece. I sat in the Soup
Kitchen fuming. I was pissed. I thought, "There was a
reason for punk, and you are it."

Here was an entire power structure—exactly the
people I was setting out to celebrate—who had never
once supported the younger people around them, or
even noticed us except as potential customers, potential fans, or a potential problem ("kids today just don't
understand"). The bookstores whose story I was trying
to tell had never been welcoming when I tried to tell
mine—Cody's had refused to even consign *Cometbus*
for the first sixteen years, Shakespeare & Co. the
first eighteen, and Moe's the first twenty-five. Local
author Julia Vinograd was a typical example of such
local, generational shortsightedness. Buying her books
wasn't enough—she acted like we owed her not just a
living but also worshipful respect, though never in a
million years would she think to ask what we were writing and working on at the next table over. Meanwhile,
she wrote poems like this:

AGAINST PUNK
It is better to light
one candle
than to praise the darkness.

I thought, that's the problem with hippies. They
can't live with themselves when the lights are out. No

wonder they're so angry at us, able to accept the darkness and even celebrate it. It would be funny, if only they hadn't taken all the rent-controlled apartments for themselves. All of us Berkeley kids had to move away in order to find a place to live.

Now here I was, back in my hometown for the holidays, with no one to light the candles with.

5

The Print Mint Split

SHAMBHALA WAS NOT THE ONLY publisher on the block. In fact, everyone but Shakespeare & Co. took a shot. Cody's came out with the debut volume of poetry by Julia Vinograd (known to some as Julia Stalingrad for her ruthless determination when making a sale). Moe's released a few records, each more bizarre than the last, culminating in Richard Milner's *The Contraceptive Puts You On*, an album of disturbingly bad comedy with one heartrending reference to fucking in Provo Park.

But it was Print Mint, the poster and framing shop, whose publishing venture was the most immediately successful and influential. Their newsprint anthology *Yellow Dog* was part of the shot-heard-round-the-world that created underground comics.

It was not the very first of the undergrounds—that distinction goes to Joel Beck, the El Sobrante boy wonder whose self-published *Lenny of Laredo* appeared in 1966. Don Donahue of Berkeley's Go Broke Press followed with *Zap* #1 in 1967 (*Zap* #0 was earlier, but delayed for a year when the originals were lost). *Yellow Dog* didn't hit the streets until early '68, but new issues kept steadily rolling off the press. In a landscape of one-shots, Print Mint proved to be the only steady publisher in the pack.

Before long, Print Mint had taken over production of *Zap* and both of Joel Beck's books. Their roster grew fast: Gilbert Shelton (of later *Freak Brothers* fame), Robert Williams, R. Crumb, and others.

On one hand, Print Mint's Don Schenker became the primary publisher for underground comics. On the other, he remained the form's biggest booster and number-one fan. A conflict of interest, for sure—but one caused, in this case, by mania rather than self-interest.

He championed the emerging artists not just for their talents but for their willingness to break taboos and speak the truth. In a 1968 *Daily Californian* article, his enthusiasm was palpable. He envisioned the underground cultural network as its own separate country with its own maps and charts, its own lore and traditions. "The heads of the American underground are its artists," he wrote, "the new cartoonists are its cartographers."

Noting that hard rock, psychedelic poster art, and underground comics were all native to the Bay Area, he saw these three mediums as "the means of mapping the geography of the new country."

Schenker was excitable but on to something. History is full of half-crazed dreamers who stumble upon their historical moment as if by accident—and so is this story. He was committed. "Don Schenker was a deeply troubled, neurotic man," remembers R. Crumb, himself something of an expert on the subject. "The Print Mint gave him a nervous breakdown."

Well, better than getting one from working at the bank.

Right? Hmmm.

At the time, there was no ready outlet for the books Schenker was printing. Comic book stores as we know them didn't exist. That institution was also just beginning, growing side by side with the new undergrounds and, like them, native to Northern California. Gary Arlington's SF Comic Book Company opened in the Mission in '67, Bud Plant's place in Grass Valley in '68. There were more titles and artists than stores. Outlets had to be created, which is what Schenker did, selling mostly to head shops.

Print Mint became a distributor for the few titles they didn't already publish, piggybacking the comics onto their already established (and thriving) poster distribution business, for which a warehouse on West Berkeley's Folger Street had been rented. The wholesale discount for the comics was set the same as for posters—60 percent—much more generous than in the regular book trade. As a result of this accident, the same disproportionate discount is still in effect, much to the chagrin of present-day comic publishers.

Naturally, the Telegraph Avenue Print Mint sold the comics they produced and promoted. So did Moe's—even putting up the money for Schenker to reprint *Zap* #1. These flew off the shelves—350 copies a day of R. Crumb's *Snatch* alone. People couldn't get enough. The comics touched a nerve that needed to be touched.

Schenker spoke of a "virus in the vitals of the American consciousness." He said: "This is how we recognize a fellow American on the street—by the look of lost delight, the loneliness in his eyes."

Conversely, the new comics reminded people of their forgotten capacity to feel delight.

The result was inevitable. Somebody called the cops. Or rather, they called themselves, as often happens, after an undercover pig bought a copy of *Snatch* at Moe's and passed it around to his squad.

The police raided Moe's, seizing 47 copies of *Horseshit*, 74 copies of *Zap #2*, and one each of *Mah Fellow Americans* by Ron Cobb and Valerie Solanas's *Scum Manifesto*.

They also seized Moe, charging him with selling obscene material. He was led away. "The balding bookseller was released on $500 bail," the *San Francisco Chronicle* reported the next day.

The *Daily Cal* also commented on Moe's pate and fate, quoting him as saying, "They wanted to get me because of *Snatch* magazine, but I'd sold out and they were disappointed."

Apparently, the earlier undercover cop had bought the very last one.

A reporter visited Shakespeare & Co. across the street to elicit a statement of fraternal support. "We're just waiting to see what the charges are," Cartwright stated valiantly, meanwhile taking his own copies of *Horseshit* off the shelf, "just in case."

Other busts followed. A show of original comic art at the Phoenix Gallery on College Avenue—run by Si Lowinsky, former manager of Print Mint's San Francisco store—was raided in November 1969, and the Schenkers themselves were arrested in the spring of 1970. Lawyers for the Phoenix opted for a jury trial and won an acquittal after the head of UC Berkeley's art museum and other bigwigs testified on the gallery's behalf. That precedent set, the Schenkers' case was thrown out of court.

Unfortunately, they had bigger problems on the way.

The Schenkers had an idea: wouldn't it be nice to have some partners? They could swap running the business—work half the year, then have half the year off.

So, they took in a guy who worked for them, a very clever, dynamic guy who had been a grape picker. He'd come to Berkeley during the grape strike to raise money for the strikers. He'd gotten married, and his wife came to work at Print Mint, too. They seemed like ideal candidates.

"And that worked for a period of time," Alice Schenker says, then laughs. "I can't say we ever got to the point where they ran the business half the year and we did the other half.

"But that eventually came to a parting of the ways. And, uh, we split the business. We'd been a little dumb about it, giving them partnership. We were a corporation, so we were legally bound. We had to come to an agreement. We came to what we thought was a reasonable settlement of splitting the business."

Bob Rita was the grape picker turned business partner, "a big, tough Samoan," according to R. Crumb. Peggy Rita was his wife. Together, they took over the publishing wing of Print Mint. They got the comics, the posters, and the Folger Street place. "Rita would be lounging around in the office with his buddies who were all tough guys like him," Crumb says. "They would all look at me as if to say, 'Who's this pencil-necked geek?'"

"Without us, they did not do all that well," says Alice. The highly ambitious but unsuccessful *Arcade* magazine (edited by Art Spiegelman and Bill Griffith) was their only lasting legacy. Many of the Print Mint titles were soon taken over by Last Gasp. Then, in a last-ditch effort to survive, the Ritas bought a press and turned to printing, one thing Print Mint had never done, despite the name. As a gesture of support, the Schenkers had some invoices made.

Alice and Don kept the retail shop on Telegraph. They went back to where they had started: mounting and framing. No more comics. And they had to change the name—the Ritas got that, too, in the breakup, since all the publishing copyrights were registered that way.

The new name fit their backward step as well as a spirit of rebirth: "the Reprint Mint."

KEN
SARACHAN

6

A Curious Dream

KEN SARACHAN WAS A twenty-year-old UC Berkeley dropout with a dream. But it was a weird dream. In it the turn-of-the-century Russian monk Rasputin came to visit him. "Sell things round and flat," Rasputin said, "and you shall be rich."

And so, Ken did. And soon he was. Filthy rich. Rich beyond belief. Eventually he owned half the Avenue. But success didn't change him. He stayed exactly the same. The same kid from Rochester with the smirk and the pizza stains on his shirt.

I remember the first time someone pointed him out. "See that fat guy outside Blondie's muttering to himself? Believe it or not, he owns the place."

It was hard to believe. Though Ken was a multi-millionaire, he looked more like a homeless guy, and coming from me that actually means something. He shunned the airs and manners that other business-men assume. He certainly didn't have a suit and tie! And there was no way to reach him through official channels—I'd tried. Thirty-five years after his arrival in Berkeley, the only way to find him was the same way you find someone who showed up last week: go up to the Ave. and see if they're hanging out.

That's how I ran into him the last week of December: he was walking out of Rasputin's while I was on my way to the park. He looked exactly the same as I remembered. If anything, he looked more the same—a caricature of himself. Flecks of spit rested on the corner of his lips. His fly was down. His glasses were crooked and his hair was a mess.

I introduced myself. He shrugged at me but didn't brush me off. And so, I followed. We headed north, angling through the swarms of undergrads.

There I was, strolling with the "Devil of Telegraph Avenue" like it was no big thing. Me and the Berkeley bogeyman, the most hated man in town, hands down, just chilling. And the strange thing was that for someone so heinous, so hated, there was something particularly likeable about the guy. That was the catch. He was an asshole, but an interesting one. That was why everyone who spoke ill of him—including the manager fired for taking one day off in seven years, to lie in a hospital nearly dead—did so with a smile. His level of evil was hilarious.

The fact was, of all people on earth, he really just didn't give a fuck. Not about you, not about what anybody thought.

It was refreshing.

Yet when I told Ken about my mission, he got misty-eyed. "I'll tell you a story about Moe," he said, then headed straight for the one subject I'd been afraid to bring up.

"In 1970, I pulled my International Harvester van into the yellow zone in front of his store. I started selling books out of the van, buying Moe's rejects. And, you know, different buyers take different books, so I'd bring in stuff every shift to sell to them, and each time they'd take a few. What one buyer passed on, another might pay good money for. I built up a huge amount of trade credit that way. Moe saw me in there getting all his best books with my trade slips, and he was curious: 'Who is this kid? What's he up to?' Instead of being mad, he thought it was cool.

"Moe loved me," Ken gushed.

However, others I'd spoken to remembered it a little differently.

"Moe hated him," said John Wong.

"Moe couldn't stand him," said Julian Segal.

"Moe decked him one time when he caught him in the dumpster," said Kent Randolph. "At least, that's what I heard."

Bob Baldock, when asked if he remembered Ken's arrival on the Avenue, said, "Yes, I do. All too clearly. He had this funky old van and he's out front going, 'I'll give you a dollar for that carton.' I guess he did pretty well with that. If he'd only been a little stylish, we would have helped him out—but he's such a morbid character. And he had a lot of attitude about Moe, and an attitude about the whole world, that was basically sneering."

At the time, all the local secondhand bookstores

carried albums. Pellucidar—the present-day Pegasus—had a great record section, and, unlike Moe's, had no compunction about kicking Ken out ("They banned me for fifteen years," he bragged). Moe's record department is something the old dealers still speak of wistfully, as if shorthand for their own youth. It was, after all, where many of them met—and met the music that became their first love. For Doris Moskowitz, it was literally where she grew up, since the children's section was also located on Moe's bottom floor. "It was like heaven," she says. "Reading, and there's Miles Davis playing. I loved it."

And right outside stood a horrible troll guarding the bridge. It was Ken, with his funky van, snatching people as they passed. He was buying not only Moe's rejects, but whatever he could get to first, waylaying customers before they could make it in the door. He bought both books and records, but had better luck with the latter, so began to specialize.

In 1971, Ken ditched the van and set up a table, becoming—by his own estimation—Telegraph's very first street vendor. He kept a copy of the Peddler's Ordinance from 1900 in his pocket to ward off the cops. Unfortunately, they read the small print, which stipulated that vendors couldn't stay stationary for more than sixty minutes. Moe had gone up against this same archaic law a decade earlier when trying to get the city to approve the kiosk he'd built in front of the Paperback Bookshop. Moe had fought but lost. Stubborn as Moe was, he wasn't half as stubborn as

Ken, who flippantly dragged his record stand up the avenue twenty feet at a time as the day passed.

Within a year, he had managed to open his own store—Rasputin's Records—while simultaneously working the street. But the next summer brought a slew of imitators—seventy-five people all trying to set up on the sidewalk. Fistfights erupted over turf. The city responded by passing a new law that legalized vending yet heavily restricted what could be sold. Only goods that were handcrafted and homemade were allowed. Candlemakers, sandalmakers, psychics—all fine. But not record sellers. Ken was legislated right out of the marketplace he'd created. But he didn't let it bother him. There were other markets to be made. He had the taste for it, and the touch.

Other hip record stores existed, like the "Leopold Stokowski Memorial Service Pavilion," one of eight collective businesses started with a grant from the Student Union at UCB. But stores like Leopold's, no matter how cool, only carried new records. Even with their cooperative structure and "longhairs only" hiring policy, they were still Cody's-like compared to Ken's cheaper and funkier shop, the only one in town that was all-used. Which isn't to suggest that Ken was Moe-like. Local engineer-producer Kevin Army remembers being tracked down by Moe because a Moe's employee had underpaid him for a Willie "the Lion" Smith LP. Such a thing would never happen with Ken. However, neither was Ken the only one in town buying on the cheap. Pellucidar gave Army the same price—five bucks—for a first edition of *Dharma Bums*, and happily watched him leave.

Ken's next venture, Blondie's, started out as a sandwich shop, named after the comic strip with the sandwich-crazed bumbling fool. Rasputin's employees—and by now there were many—could walk behind the counter and fix their own sandwiches for free. But something was missing. Ken remembered Rasputin. He began to scheme. There was a pizzeria in the Village Mall courtyard, a small family place. Their pizza was delicious, but the location was too far afield for most students to go. There was a worker there named Joe Taylor. Ken befriended him and promised him a job for life if he would steal the sauce recipe and come work for Ken—and Joe agreed.

So, Blondie's phased out the sandwiches and turned into a pizza place. As terrible and inedible as it was, the competition (Fat Slice—started with a Blondie's manager and chef) proved even worse, and students had to get pizza somewhere, since living off pizza for three and a half years was part of the myth they would speak of later when recounting their early hardships. A long line formed out the door.

At the same time that Blondie's changed, the book-stores started phasing out their records. Rasputin's had taken the main share of the market, and continued to expand. Whatever crumbs were left were spread thin between the score of smaller, specialized used stores that had sprouted up.

Moe's stock of records went to Richard Brown,

the weathered veteran of Moe's record department, who teamed up with Barry Berrigan (of Berrigan's Records) to open a jazz-specialty store on Piedmont called Berrigan & Brown's. Like all partners in this tale, they ended up having a bad falling out and split into two stores—Berrigan's and DBA Brown—both located on the same small stretch of Claremont. Unlike most of the other partners, they still talked and their competition was friendly. Regardless, both shops are now gone, as is Leopold's, the only record store that had been on the Avenue longer than Rasputin's. (Of the original eight collectives, only the bike shop Missing Link remains.) Longtime Rasputin's manager Eric Yee remembers breaking the news to Ken:

"When I told him Leopold's was closing, this huge smile appeared on his face. I'd never seen him so happy."

As for Ken and his dream, we'll return to them momentarily. But for those of you who can't sleep and are lucky enough to find yourself on the Avenue in the wee hours, those beautiful, blessed hours between nighttime and day, come lean with me against the Bank of America building and watch as an unlikely figure emerges from the twilight mist: a short, grumpy, pot-bellied Black man wearing a T-shirt that reads, in large letters, "Fuck you!"

It's Joe Taylor, going to work at Blondie's as he has every morning for the past twenty-seven years.

By now you'd think he'd have saved up enough money to retire, and you'd be right. He's even bought a piece of land—some prime waterfront property on a tropical island on which to spend his old age. Get off his feet and this fucking street and go lie on the beach. Unfortunately, the tropical island paradise in question—Fiji—is on the brink of civil war, with no end to the crisis in sight.

And so he waits, mixing the sauce and marking time.

KATHY SOLIAH

7

I Am the SLA

IN THE EARLY MORNING of May 17, 1974, the majority of the Symbionese Liberation Army was surrounded by the LAPD and killed in the ensuing firefight. In Berkeley there were mixed feelings. Most leftists considered the SLA adventurist if not downright insane. Of the local guerrilla armies—and there were enough to make alphabet soup—the SLA stood out only as the most violent and most daring. But, because of the latter, there was a degree of sympathy for the group, and not-uncritical support.

Locally, the fallen SLA members were missed less as comrades—they had never been political "heavies"— than as familiar faces around town. Nancy Ling Perry had worked at the juice stand on Sproul Plaza, Patricia Soltysik at the main library, and Camilla Hall doing landscaping at Lake Temescal. Among the mourners were former lovers, neighbors, and others whose brief connections with the SLA had come to be a liability and something of an embarrassment.

A memorial rally was held at Ho Chi Minh Park. A large crowd gathered, half reporters and half under-cover police. Kathy Soliah, the event's main organizer, had been best friends with Angela Atwood, another of the SLA dead. Soliah's impassioned speech was remembered by everyone present, though remembered differently. One account quotes her as saying, "Keep fighting! I'm with you! We're with you!" Another has her leading a chant: "We are the SLA! I am the SLA!"

Of course, no one took her words seriously, much less literally. No one except the SLA themselves, holed up in a nearby safehouse with enough guns and bombs to blow up Fort Knox. They got the morning paper and read it just like everyone else.

There were only three SLA members left: Emily and Bill Harris, and the kidnapped heiress turned revolutionary gun moll, Patty Hearst. It was only by accident that they had missed getting killed in LA along with their comrades. Now they were broke and hungry and needed help. This Soliah woman seemed like their best bet.

Two weeks after the rally, Kathy Soliah was at work, running the register at a bookstore near the UC Berkeley campus. A woman approached, and Soliah recognized her right away even though they had never met. It was Emily Harris in a grey wig. "Would you be good enough to throw this away for me, please?" Emily asked, handing her a note. "Meet me at the church," it read.

Soliah went on break and ran around the corner to where Emily was waiting. After a quick conference, they agreed to meet again the following night at an Oakland drive-in where *The Sting* was playing. Soliah and her boyfriend Jim Kilgore parked in the adjacent lot, under the screen showing a porno called *Teacher's Pet*. Patty Hearst and Emily and Bill Harris climbed into the backseat and everyone hugged and kissed as if they'd known each other for years.

From that meeting, the SLA received a new lease on life. According to Soliah—and statements from Emily Harris bear this out—she never actually joined the group, only provided support. But the support was considerable. With Soliah came a dedicated, tight-knit crew that included her younger brother and sister. They were the ones who leased the safehouses, drove the getaway cars, and seem to have taken part in more of the "armed propaganda" than any of the official SLA members. Successful bombing targets included ITT, Dean Witter, General Motors, PG&E, the Air Force, the State Parole Board, the Bureau of Indian Affairs, San Quentin Prison, and two Alameda County Sheriff vehicles. Besides all of that, they stole cars and robbed banks—and helped put out the underground paper *Dragon*, whose PO box was but a few feet from mine.

Of all these actions, none caused a single injury— until the ill-fated Carmichael bank job where Myrna Opsahl, a nurse depositing the collection money from her church, was killed. (Emily Harris has since been convicted of her accidental death.)

All the while, the new cadre kept their day jobs. Half of the SLA entourage had their own housepainting company. Kathy Soliah waitressed at a restaurant in the Sir Francis Drake Hotel, under the pseudonym

"Kathleen Anger." Tipped off ahead of time, she walked off the job right before the FBI showed up.

When Patty Hearst and Emily and Bill Harris were caught in September 1975, most of the SLA "second team" escaped and went underground. Soliah and Kilgore made it to St. Paul before splitting up— Kilgore to Zimbabwe (and it wasn't until 2004 that he was discovered and extradited from South Africa).

Soliah—under the alias Sara Jane Olson—stayed in the Twin Cities and remained active in progressive causes. She was part of the Mayday bookstore collective, and helped found *Arise!*, an anti-racist newspaper that grew out of the anti-apartheid struggle (and took its name from a poem by the late, great Midwestern author Meridel Le Sueur). *Arise!* also opened an office that ran educational programs. After the *Arise!* faction was purged from Mayday in the early '90s, they opened their own bookstore.

When Soliah was busted in 1999, those of us who'd spent time at both Mayday and Arise! were shocked: a real revolutionary had been right there in our midst, packing boxes with the Women's Prisoner Book Project and taking our fanzines on consignment. She was still involved, and taking a supporting role rather than resting on her laurels. Hardly the picture of the repentant, washed-up '60s radical that the media repeats again and again. But then again, who is?

And still, the burning question remained, more so than ever: which Berkeley bookstore did she work at in 1974? The curiosity was killing me.

Could it be Cody's? I asked Pat Cody, but to her the story was unfamiliar. She did confirm that Mario Savio worked there part-time.

Jon Wobber at Shakespeare & Co. didn't recognize the name, but said that Philip K. Dick was rumored to have worked at the store. Good rumor—but unsubstantiated, he admits.

John Wong at Moe's didn't remember any Kathy Soliah, and said he would have had she been there, since there were so few women who worked at Moe's.

That was yet another burning question, and one I didn't even have to bring up: why Moe's never hired women.

"Well," Wong replied, "the ones we did have were awful."

Ouch!

But his words didn't come as a big surprise. Moe's had always had a macho vibe, an ever-present male energy that was arrogant and a little ugly. And no wonder, since Moe himself was a pig. Not a chauvinist pig, but a pig nonetheless—loud and oafish, holding court in a pen of his own crap, with a big cigar in his mouth.

I remember coming into Moe's as a kid, and seeing him behind the counter, feeling like I was at the zoo. Here was the perfect example of the kind of man you didn't want to grow up to be: overburdened and overbearing, always needing to be the center of attention. Of course, growing up, you pick and choose from the different archetypes available, and there was much that was fascinating about the dynamic energy of Moe and the men who surrounded him. But I wanted to be loved by women. Whenever there weren't any in sight, it seemed like a bad sign. I could have used other role models, like Audrey Goodfriend—Moe's matchmaker and, later, bookkeeper—with her terrific stories of Italian anarchists exiled by Mussolini who settled in the small, outlying towns of the Bay Area (Los Gatos, Petaluma, Pleasanton) to raise orchards and were still there having anarchist picnics until the late '80s! But Audrey was unavailable, invisible, kept in the back.

Bob Baldock claims that Moe's theatricality was only an act to cover his more sensitive side. Probably so, but so what? After a while, your cover is no excuse. Couldn't he have at least hired the SLA? An (almost) all-woman army might have balanced things out at Moe's and kept the place from being so uptight.

Finally, I was ready to throw in the towel on my search when a letter arrived at my PO box from an unlikely source: Kathy Soliah herself.

"Dear Aaron," she wrote.

"What a delightful surprise to get your letter. It's great to get a surprise while in prison that is enjoyable.

"As for the Telegraph Business District history, I'm not *that* old. I didn't reach the Bay Area to live until 1970. I did work in one of the bookstores. Actually, I was working there when Emily Harris, after the police massacre of the majority of the SLA members in Los Angeles, showed up in disguise seeking help. And—well—the rest is history."

And the bookstore—was it Moe's? Cody's? Shakespeare & Co.?

No. None of the above. It was the Campus Textbook Exchange on Bancroft. The lousy textbook place that none but the lowliest undergrad would ever enter.

Alas.

8

Rag Theater

CHANGES WERE AFOOT ON the Ave. People talked about Telegraph in doomsday terms. They looked out the window and saw the world ending. The chickens had come home to roost.

"It was like the aftermath of some kind of nuclear war," says Shambhala's Michael Fagan. "It was totally blown away and seedy and crummy and filled with doped-up and really nasty street people. It was crazy. The whole place looked like a camp.

"Berkeley was having huge demonstrations that brought police, the National Guard finally, barbed wire, the whole thing. We weren't interested in provoking that kind of stuff. That didn't benefit the bookstore because nobody wanted to come downtown."

Fagan went on, as if to make sure I understood that the '60s weren't his fault—nor was the fallout that followed.

Shambhala wasn't a radical bookstore, he emphasized. Those kinds of politics just create polarization and problems.

Got it.

Besides, he and Bercholz had always had an

apocalyptic view of the Bay Area. In 1969 they had seriously considered leaving California and, if possible, the country. The plan was to franchise out the bookstore then buy a building in Vancouver and start a new store there. Had they done it—he laughs—they could have retired early, cashing in on the real estate boom that hit Vancouver five years later.

But things don't always work out the way you planned.

Now it was 1975 and Fagan, the native Northern Californian, just couldn't take it anymore. "I kept on getting messages," he recalls. "The sky, rocks. Everything was saying, 'Get out of here.'"

So he sold his share of Shambhala and moved to New Mexico, breaking up the "society of one" and perhaps regretting ever coming up with such a self-fulfilling phrase. The lawyer handling the dissolution of the partnership insisted on one condition: anonymity. Fagan's settlement was so skimpy that the lawyer feared he'd never work again were it known that he handled the case.

But it paid off in other ways: Fagan and Bercholz remained friends for life.

Bercholz fled Telegraph soon afterwards, in 1976, taking the whole publishing operation with him to Boulder. "There's an illusion in Berkeley that you're in the forefront of thought," he explained, "and it's just an illusion."

Fair enough. But, Boulder? I must refrain from comment, since snide comments about Boulder could fill another book—or add enough pages to this one to force the long-delayed increase in price (whoops, too late).

Bercholz retained ownership of the Berkeley store, leaving it in the care of a succession of employee-managers. It continued to thrive, end of the world on the doorstep or not. (In fact, paranoia and apocalypse are always good business for a metaphysical-theological shop.)

Anyway, Bercholz and Fagan weren't the only ones abandoning ship. As early as 1968, Pat Cody was complaining about the changing face of Telegraph. There was "less flower children . . . more paranoia, permanent dropouts, greater use and abuse of drugs."

By 1970, she and Fred were considering selling the store, largely in response to their employees' attempt to unionize. "The store may be for sale," Fred told the staff, "so we can't agree to anything that might limit our options."

Fred launched into negotiations with prospective buyers in 1974—for real, this time—and in 1977 a deal was sealed. Pat and Fred departed Telegraph, leaving their shop in other, younger hands.

The former site of the Telegraph Hilton was now a vacant lot separating Cody's from Moe's. The lore of that lot and the hotel's last years could also fill a book of its own. Bob Baldock remembers acid casualties walking out windows and splattering on the sidewalk below. Alice Schenker describes the building's owner, a former missionary in Africa, as the "stingiest, most uncooperative guy you could ever run into." During one demonstration, Jerry Rubin addressed the crowd on Telegraph from one of the Hilton balconies. The landlord was so incensed, says Alice, that he busted into the room to stop Rubin from speaking, but was set upon by hippies who locked him in a closet for the duration of Rubin's speech.

Larry Livermore, founder of Lookout Records, remembers a bell at the top of the Hilton's stairs that served as the Avenue's fire alarm. Ring it and the building would empty out into the street to riot. "It's riot time, let's drop some sunshine and throw some bricks!" was the Hilton's call to arms.

According to Pat Cody's autobiography, the final straw for the Hilton came early—in 1965, when Cody's moved out. After that, it housed "successive enterprises, each one seedier than the one before." Like many of Pat's comments, this was a not-so-veiled dig at Moe's, which took Cody's place. "At the end," she writes, "it became a hangout for drug users."

The larger truth seems both more complicated and more colorful. Among the businesses that followed Moe's was Rag Theater, a secondhand clothing shop which inspired a beautiful book of photographs by the same name, documenting the early '70s Telegraph street scene, much of which thrived right outside its doors. A teenage gang called the Red Rockets leaned in the entryway, dressed in matching satin jackets and flanked by their younger, pre-teen auxiliary, the Mini-Mob. Others, including a young Larry Livermore, strutted up and down the block in elaborate costume and makeup in a sort of protoglam parade, moved by the same spirit as Rag Theater—one of playful reinvention. Thrift stores had always existed, but Rag Theater was perhaps the first place to turn secondhand into hip.

After the building was razed, the lot served as a flea market site.

Then, in 1977, Barb bought the property. While others were packing up, Moe's decided to stay and expand. Every business on the block scratched the address off their letterhead as construction began. Time for yet another round of musical chairs—the old Moskowitz shuffle—as each of Barb's tenants moved one step to the left, into bigger and better quarters once again.

Around the corner on Dwight Way was the most recent Moe's offshoot—and further proof that when it came to bad ideas, Moe just couldn't say no. The question is, why did so many of these bad ideas turn out so good? We'll overlook Moe's sponsorship of the elusive Chinese rock band, and "Moe's Behind," the short-lived cafe in back of the building, with its door in the drama section. Everything else backed by Moe and Barb blossomed. Each project evolved into a huge success, even if awkward at first, and this newest venture was no exception. In comparison, Cody's and Shakespeare & Co. produced no offspring at all. The former did have one side project early on, an outlet for hiking and mountaineering supplies. A good idea, too, and one ahead of its time—but Cody's dropped it cold after just a couple months.

Joe Fischer, longtime Moe's staffer, was given the storefront on Dwight to house his specialty: Indonesian studies. He called it "More Moe's."

Not surprisingly, business was slow.

So Bob Baldock came in, employing what he calls the "de Tocqueville idea": that a bookstore, like a society, needs both high and low—the common as well as the one-of-a-kind.

Baldock himself is something of a mixed bag—a guy who speaks with equal reverence for Che Guevara and Chez Panisse. He filled More Moe's with what he dismissively calls "the Republican section": books on art, architecture, and photography.

Regardless, his overhaul of the store was a runaway success. When construction on the Telegraph Hilton site was complete, More Moe's moved into the top floor of the new building, becoming Moe's much-vaunted art and antiquarian department. Cartesian Books—one store with no Moe's relation—took over the vacant space on Dwight.

Across the street sat Cartwright—on a stool by the door of Shakespeare & Co., as if anxious to escape. As always, he was jealous of his former partner's success. He had managed to expand his own store, but only by about ten feet. Now his inferiority complex was piqued by Moe's growing eminence when it came to art books. In response, Cartwright bought some art books of his own to showcase. One was about the "Running Fence" project by Christo, the much-hyped and much-hated artist whose giant umbrellas were always falling and killing people, and whose fabric "wraps" threatened to strangle sheep. The book, which was very expensive, came with an actual piece of the fence.

However, Cartwright couldn't sell it. No one cared. Shakespeare & Co. didn't have the clientele to support books of that kind.

Shakespeare & Co. employee Robert Eliason says Cartwright kept marking the book down for months. Finally, a customer came in and asked to see it. Cartwright went into his sales pitch and the customer seemed hooked—but left after asking to have it put it on hold.

Cartwright was moaning about how his one chance to sell the book had just walked out the door. Then, just before closing, the customer came back. Cartwright was so overjoyed that he sold the book at cost, with no tax, which meant actually at a loss.

And as soon as the guy had left, Cartwright turned to Eliason.

"That was easy," he said. "We should order another one."

BALDOCK ON RIGHT, BIVINS ON LEFT, WITH TWO EMPLOYEES

9

The Heart of a Revolutionary

WHEN I FIRST CONTACTED Bob Baldock, it was just to confirm one small fact.

I'd pored over newspaper accounts of Moe's Books, including more than a few on Baldock, Moe's right-hand man. Every report was alike—the same tired anecdotes repeated over and over, each time with less accuracy and punch.

Only one diverted from the oft-repeated myths. In it, this line caught my eye: "Baldock left a college scholarship in baseball at Ohio University and headed south for Cuba; he and a companion defied the customs laws of the Cuban government and hitchhiked 700 miles to the village of Bayamo where they joined the forces of Fidel Castro and his 'July 26 Movement' in the Sierra Maestra Mountains."

I was floored. Surely, this was a misprint or a misunderstanding. How else could such a bombshell go unmentioned in all the other reports? Besides, the same article lost all credibility when it referred to Olympia Press as "Olympic."

Baldock suggested we meet in person. Have coffee and a real conversation—a chance to answer that question and any others that might come up. For our rendezvous, he picked a cafe on Shattuck one block from Black Oak Books.

"I'm tall and usually slightly disheveled or lost-looking," I told him, so he'd know where to look.

"I'm a slouching 6'4", often scowling uncertainly," he fired back.

On the chosen day, I approached the cafe with apprehension. Last time I'd been there, it was a gas station. Admittedly, more than twenty years had passed, but I was still waiting to see how the "new" place turned out. Inside, the room was packed—with no one under 6'2" or in a good mood. Luckily, I'd seen old photos of Baldock and recognized him at once.

While I turned on the tape, he cut to the chase. He confirmed his trip to Cuba, comparing it to that of the Abraham Lincoln Brigade members who fought against Franco in Spain.

"In Cuba," he said, "there were only two of us who went from the mainland. We went together. The only other North Americans in the Sierra were sons of naval personnel at Guantanamo who went up into the mountains for a while."

Again, I was stunned. But, overexcited, I spoke too soon and Baldock backed off. When I asked if the Guantanamo kids had fought or just provided behind-the-lines support, he carefully measured his response.

"Well," he said, "one thing or another."

Opinions on the present situation at Guantanamo were more forthcoming. "Fidel's attitude towards torture, and what we did while I was there in terms of prisoners, was just about the sacred antithesis of what the US is now doing. We made the prisoners love us. Not in any funky way, but in a real way, and by very concrete, pragmatic methods. And it really worked. It was a way of carrying out what Che had written and said a number of times: 'The heart of a revolutionary has to be driven mostly by love.' Not hatred, not revenge, not justice, not social peace, but love. That simple."

I sat there in the former gas station thinking, "Did he say 'we'? Wow." But also, "So, what the hell brought you here?" From Cuba to a North Berkeley cafe seemed an unlikely if not wrong turn, though I'd had worse. Here at least the coffee was good.

Slowly he filled in the details.

Baldock's time with the guerrillas, though life-changing, was brief, cut short by an acute case of amoebic dysentery. He dropped from 178 pounds to 110 in just two months. If not for considerable efforts and risks taken by Fidel himself, Baldock might not have survived.

"I'd been traveling with Fidel's personal troops for a long time," he recalls, "and however stupid and innocent I was, I did know a lot of things, and would have been a danger to them had I been grabbed and caught, no question about it. But he moved me, largely through church facilities, down the 700 miles of the island and into the Havana airport and out on a plane. And the other guy, my friend Bill McGiven, we got out together."

When I asked if McGiven got dysentery too, Baldock growled.

"No, he didn't have dysentery, the swine. He stayed perfectly well all the way through—cheerful and buoyant, doing what he did. He was the one who took photographs."

McGiven's photos, paired with Baldock's written notes, offered an intimate, firsthand account of the Cuban revolution, a view unavailable to anyone else in the West. Their portrait of the nascent movement took on even more importance when, just six months later, Castro's forces emerged victorious. UPI bought the lot, with part-payment being a scholarship to journalism school for Baldock. Off to NYU he went—back, actually, since he'd been there already for two years in between Ohio and the armed struggle.

In New York, he worked at two bookstores, one on Bleecker and one at Sheridan Square (the aforementioned pool-of-live-penguins place); also at two publishers, Macmillan and Doubleday, at the first as copyeditor and at the second boiling down bestsellers for abridged editions abroad. Baldock admits a certain sadistic glee at trimming off unimportant subplots and "yards of bad prose." (Irving Stone's *The Agony and the Ecstasy* lost the most, emerging from the edit like Baldock from Havana.)

Journalism proved to be a wash, but Baldock was also working on his own fiction. One piece won an *Olympia Review* contest, the prize for which needed to be collected in person. Once the State Department returned his confiscated passport, he left for Paris (with a long stay en route in southern Spain). There, Olympia Press took him on as staff, and Anaïs Nin found him and his then-wife a really nice apartment. Baldock kept writing: two novels and change.

"And so, life was good," he says. The thousand-dollar prize was never paid, but why complain?

From Paris, the couple came to Berkeley, where Baldock enters our story in earnest. He took a job at SLA Books (Campus Textbook Exchange) but found it dull. One day at lunch, he wandered into Moe's, where the proprietor was just getting set up, putting books on the shelves of his still-empty shop. Baldock asked to be hired and was, on the spot.

He was the first of a group of young men to arrive and find in Moe's a sort of home. Starting with Baldock, Moe treated these men partly like sidekicks and partly like sons. He gave them full responsibility and support. In return, they built up the bookstore so that its content matched its force of character. It was a good deal for everyone.

They became Moe's lieutenants, and Baldock, first lieutenant.

It was Baldock who introduced new books into Moe's, reasoning that people were more likely to bring in their quality libraries if hot-off-the-press titles were available in trade. (Cody's and Moe's had long since dropped their all-paperback rule.) Remainders were also added. But the main addition was in staff. That, more than any of the physical expansions, was what caused Moe's to grow.

Each new arrival into the group brought his own particular expertise and intensity, and, like Moe himself, something of an overabundance of personality.

Baldock was stormy, wry, and engaging—as should already be obvious. He knew the "Republican section" and had a decent handle on fiction and poetry. Bob Brown, politely described as "not noticeably extroverted," was the classics guy, a serious scholar of Latin and French. Richard Brown (no relation) was the amiable, unashamed ex-addict who ran the used record department. John Wong was a poker-faced sharpie, hired with no bookstore experience—and over Baldock's objections—because of the fondness he shared with Moe for shooting pool. (Richard Brown was a hustler, too, having once run the pool hall at the Berkeley Bowl back when the place was still a bowling alley.)

There was also Joe Fischer, the career shelver with a sideline in Indonesian studies, even-tempered Gene "Gino" Barone, and Herb Bivins, the one person no one on earth speaks badly about (though neither do they have anything particularly interesting to say).

A cast of thousands passed through the store but didn't make a dent. It was these men who were the pillars of the place—plus the sole woman, Audrey Goodfriend—and the main reason for its success. Without them, Moe was just a ringleader without a show, standing behind the counter puffing on a Macanudo and telling bad jokes. Plus, there was the fact that he didn't know much about books.

He realized all this, which is why he promised to give his employees the store. Which leads us to the second half of the Bob Baldock Story.

Young men get old and have kids of their own. Baldock did, Bob Brown too. Old cigar-smoking men get older and have heart attacks. Moe did, twice. Yet years passed with the same vague promise and no plan in action or on paper. Baldock, Moe's faithful sidekick, was no longer the starry-eyed kid he'd been when he first wandered in. Eighteen years had passed, all of them at Moe's Books. He began to smolder.

"Moe had promised for a long time to make us—the people who'd been there a long time—partners," Baldock says. "Because, frankly, the guy had already had a heart attack or two. He goes, and you're left at the mercies—if they exist—of a very fickle wife. Where's the job security there?

"There were some pragmatics involved. I had a couple of kids. Brown had a kid. We're not fools. We'd watched unions get destroyed. We'd watched what happened to the labor movement in this country. We wanted something of our own.

"And when Moe, the one thing he did in his life that I know of that was really dishonest, he got talked out of having it be a profit-sharing store. And at that point I thought, 'We've got to do something different.'"

Moe's daughter Doris—the present owner—was just graduating from high school at the time. "I don't know what my father's intentions were," she says. "I know what my mother's intentions were (laughs).

That's a funny way to say it, but she believed that I needed to be here and that I was the kind of person to do it, and I was willing to do it, and that it needed to stay in the family. Moe's decision didn't have anything to do with me. But it was finally decided, I think both my parents decided that it wasn't going to work as a collective. I think the staff here wishes that had happened, and it would've been really nice, but . . ."

She trailed off on that note, as would any business owner when faced with that sticky subject—one, incidentally, that it's never too late to rectify and resolve.

However, most people don't view Baldock and Brown as the victims of a broken promise made by their beloved mentor and boss. Instead, they are usually talked about as ungrateful thieves who took all the best stock when leaving to start their own store, and broke Moe's heart in the process. The much-told story is that Baldock and Brown went and bought books for their own store-in-the-making on Moe's time and on Moe's dime.

But, to be fair, I didn't bring this up with Baldock and give him a chance to clear his name.

Suffice to say, the perception remains. When Baldock and Brown left, their new store was known as "the best of Moe's" for more reasons than one.

DON PRETARI + BOB BROWN

10

It Came from Walnut Square

A PLAN BEGAN TO FORM as if by accident. While Baldock and Brown were gathering steam—and perhaps stock—for a store of their own, other factors stepped in to guide their hand.

Whispering in one ear were friends like David Lance Goines, the Free Speech Movement printer and legendary poster maker (famous from Shattuck Avenue all the way to Grizzly Peak). An icepick-wielding man had spooked—though not harmed—Goines one night on Haste, and now he ("like thousands of others") completely avoided the Telegraph area. What was needed, he said, was an excellent bookstore in North Berkeley.

Whispering in the other ear were some publishers' reps with insider information about a couple of warehouses in LA packed to the roof with good books that could be had for a song—by anyone but Moe, who they hated.

It didn't take much to convince Baldock and Brown. They, too, were sick of the Ave.—of the acid casualties as well as the perennial, predictable student texts that flowed back and forth across the counter.

They dreamed of a shop where people could gather without fear of getting tear-gassed or the windows getting smashed.

The deciding factor was the appearance of something rarer than a *Gravity's Rainbow* first: a sympathetic landlord. His offer included a year's free rent.

The other remaining lieutenants were summoned and asked to join. John Wong and Gene Barone said no—less out of loyalty than a feeling that even at a new store their place at the bottom of the pecking order would be the same. Don Pretari, the newest and youngest of Moe's hires (yet already an expert in linguistics and mathematics) said yes. Herb Bivins stayed on the fence. He remained at Moe's—some say as a spy—for six months before joining Baldock, Brown, and Pretari. Most likely, he just wanted to be sure the new venture was a success before cashing in his chips.

When it came to choosing a name, the new partners agreed: it should reflect the quality of the books rather than the qualities of the proprietors. Berkeley didn't need another Cody's or Moe's—top-heavy structures that rested on the decisions and ego of one man. They picked a deliberately neutral name to downplay their own personalities and roles.

On Labor Day, 1983, Black Oak Books opened. Friends and family were still laying tile and hurrying to fill the shelves as well-wishers from the neighborhood wandered in. Alice Waters, star chef of nearby Chez Panisse, came in to extend a neighborly welcome. Hank

Rubin, another Berkeley restaurateur (and Abraham Lincoln Brigade veteran) brought his personal library. Moe even came, smoking a cigar in the new store as a sort of christening. He was troubled by the defection—personally more than professionally—but gave them his blessings.

Black Oak's owners, while speaking reverently about their old boss, emphasized the differences between their new endeavor and Moe's. Black Oak was spacious, with colorful Mexican tiles and tapestries, skylights, and a garden out back. Moe's resembled "a penal reform center in Kansas." Black Oak offered comfortable chairs and a public bathroom for all to use. To Baldock, this was a political statement (to Baldock, all things are). How could it be that in Berkeley, a city with the world's first organization run by and for people with disabilities (the Center for Independent Living), bookstores didn't even have a place to sit down?

Baldock spoke emphatically about the importance of an environment where ideas could be exchanged. A community center, more casual than a classroom but without stooping so low as to become a pick-up spot.

Baldock was the one doing all the talking. The other partners were conspicuously—maybe purposely—silent. Pretari only piped up when it came to Black Oak's reading series, pointing out that along with fiction authors, writers on subjects like science, history, and philosophy would be featured. Prior to this, no other local store had readings at all, except a few at Cody's strictly for poetry. Cody's only other in-store events were book signings, better suited for fans of athletes than those of authors.

At Black Oak, writers could finally address and engage their audiences in person. The shelves were mounted on rolling casters so they could be pushed aside to accommodate large crowds—which soon arrived to see J.M. Coetzee, Oliver Sacks, and others.

One last distinction for Black Oak was its selection. While aiming to cover a wide variety of interests, it also sought to be more discriminating: only the cleanest books, only the finest titles. Of course this translated as "only the haughtiest attitudes, only the highest prices," a description that perfectly fit and still applies. In comparison, Moe's was cluttered (muddled) and Shakespeare & Co. musty (straight-up cruddy). Both were considerably cheaper, however, verging on affordable.

The only bookstore that seemed threatened by the new kid in town was Cody's. "I'd never use the word rivalry," said manager Melissa Mytinger, claiming that no changes would be made in response to the opening of Black Oak—while elsewhere announcing that Cody's was starting a reading series of its own.

Baldock was generous in his reply: "If it comes to a bar brawl, we'll be on Cody's side." Not, presumably, against Moe's, but against the larger forces of ignorance in the world. "We're like musicians in a jazz group," he said, "trying to blow a riff that's going to bring something even better out of the guy on sax and the woman on trumpet. It's the overall sound we're looking for. It's the final music."

Fine words. And now, for a change of tune, a solo from the trumpet section:

"They're taking the best books from our store, they're pricing them up across town in a frou-frou neighborhood, you know what I'm saying?"

That's Doris Moskowitz blowing now, and she's speaking not of the original, alleged looting of Moe's, but of the fact that twenty years later Bob Brown still had the audacity to come by regularly and use his old employee discount to take whatever good books might still be left. More particularly, she is demonstrating the Berkeley tendency to Balkanize our little city. Yes, Doris, we dig it. Outsiders may view Berkeley as a country of its own, but insiders think of it as nine separate war zones: Telegraph, Northside, West Berkeley, the Hills, the Flats, Ashby BART, North Berkeley, fucking Fourth Street, and Downtown. (The separate country is the common enemy smack dab in the middle: UCB.) To a Flatlander, the Berkeley Hills may feel as remote as Mount Everest. To an Elmwood resident, the glorious waterfront may seem as distant and dangerous as the Middle Ages. Speculation as to how far UCB students will venture off campus has become something of a sport. Fred Cody reported spotting them crossing Bancroft in the mid-'60s. In the anything-goes excesses of the late '60s, they were seen by Julia Stalingrad pushing as far south as Haste. The '80s saw a retreat back to Durant. "There's a feeling now that the Med is somewhere in the wilds," Stalingrad said. Across the street from the Med, Moe agreed: undergrads found the three and a half blocks between his store and campus too far to walk.

Imagine, if you will, a war of attrition, a cultural and economic impasse in which three and a half blocks make a world of difference. Then picture Bob Brown, with a truck full of discounted books, making the impossible two-mile trek to North Berkeley. He may as well have been taking looted gold to Switzerland, if you'll pardon the (fairly accurate) comparison. In fact, Black Oak's cardinal sin may have not been leaving Moe's in the first place, but where they chose to go. A newspaper account of Black Oak's opening describes their "Gourmet Ghetto" location as ideal, "surrounded by hillside warrens of professorial households and gentrifying flatlands full of literary gluttons."

Having only recently quit my job as Green Day apologist, I'm not eager to take on the equally thankless, hopeless job of North Berkeley apologist. Let me suggest, however, that this picture is not complete. Where are the *Classified Flea Market*-reading substitute teachers nodding off on the church steps while, kitty-corner, flies buzz around SSI wackos falling out of their pants in front of Peet's? Where is the Sunday crowd at Live Oak Park, running from muggers, flashers, and mimes? Dammit, I know my North Berkeley, and can attest to the fact that all was not upscale in the year of Black Oak's opening, for I was up the street at Hebrew school three times a week. Even within that tiny hamlet, two different tendencies were at war, fighting door-to-door. Sadly, the weapons that seemed most promising for our side—acid, SSI, and rent control— were what turned the tide against us in the end. It was the recipe that created a monster beyond our most far-flung fears.

It's a sad history—the Battle of North Berkeley— one from which Baldock emerged a casualty and I a refugee. It started with a population of well-educated, drug-addled young people in the early '70s. Many had Section 8 apartments, and the rest paid next to nothing thanks to progressive rent control laws. Most were childless and without dependents, so the majority of their income (or SSI check) was disposable ("discretionary," as they like to say). At the same time, small cottage businesses sprouted up in the area, shops and restaurants employing the '60s ethos by keeping everything handmade, healthy, and fresh. At least a few were collectives: the Juice Bar, the Cheese Board, plus the North Berkeley branch of the Co-op and the separate Co-op bookstore, pharmacy, and hardware stores.

Perfect, right?

But not so fast.

What happens when a bunch of hippies have the best things in the world right in the palms of their hands? They start to feel smug. Their tastes grow "refined." They become snobs—and rich, to boot, at least those who've managed to purchase some property before the housing boom. They sip wine while watching the property values climb, living off the interest on their accounts at the Co-op Credit Union.

Oh, if I'd I known then what I know now, I'd have dropped a bomb right at Shattuck and Vine.

The whole North Berkeley aesthetic was copied elsewhere: the refined tastes, the discretionary income and vaguely progressive cultural trappings, though without the SSI and rent control underpinnings. Three partners came to train at Peet's Coffee before opening their own store in Seattle with the same techniques and same beans—the name of which, now on every corner, is too horrible to even mention. Chez Panisse, another Gourmet Ghetto landmark, spawned a thousand fancy imitations. Chef Alice Waters's "Food Revolution" turned out to be the only exportable North Berkeley movement (one that Baldock likens, incidentally, to Moe's influence on the buying and selling of used books).

Some say we even invented the name: the use of the word "yuppie" in an early '80s *East Bay Express* column may have been the first.

Ironically, the mutant strain—the Berkeley Frankenstein—raged all across the country before it ever came home to visit the folks. When it finally did, it was salt in our wounds. The whole Co-op system went belly-up in 1986; the ridiculously bourgie supermarket chain Andronico's swept up nearly all of its locations and took its place.

It was into this milieu and during this time that Black Oak arrived—though not without its own internal strife. From the beginning, Baldock had been spouting off to the press about making Black Oak a collective. That insistence became a sore point with his partners as time wore on, especially as Baldock became increasingly radicalized—falling in love with a Sandinista, going to Nicaragua, and reconnecting with his Cuban roots.

Black Oak's internal battle mirrored the larger battle in the neighborhood and the city itself, the Left moving to the left and the rich moving to the right ("Other people want the gardening and the cookbooks up front, and some of us don't," he said). When Baldock brought in Sandinistas and people from El Salvador to speak about their plights, the fire department and police arrived. It was as close to tear gas and broken glass as North Berkeley was likely to see. The IRS suddenly wanted to take a look—two looks, three looks—into Black Oak's financial records. "It was bad," Baldock says. "And I wouldn't back down."

The coup came in 1989 when Baldock was in Washington, DC, at the American Booksellers convention, giving an acceptance speech for an award on behalf of Eduardo Galeano. When he returned, he was told, "Meet with the lawyer. You're out. Give us your keys."

Cody and Moe had both known one thing: with your name on the door, it's hard to get fired. Turns out that top-heavy, ego-driven structures can exist even easier within vaguely named entities to which no one person has to answer.

Brown ended up sole owner of Black Oak after outmaneuvering and outlasting all of his former partners (reportedly a multimillionaire, he bought out Pretari in 2007 for one dollar). However, by that point Black Oak was a complete mess. Their expansion into SF in the '90s proved disastrous—both SF locations were failures and their stock had to be sold off to Powell's, Portland's megastore, the ever-looming black cloud on the bookselling horizon. Pretari, before his departure, blamed the decline of North Berkeley for their woes. The customers, he said, had all moved to Fourth Street or Solano Avenue.

Brown sold the store in June 2008 with no one to blame but himself.

The media cried a river, lamenting "the end of the independent bookstore," not bothering to note that the number of bookstores in Berkeley is actually at an all-time high—reportedly the highest per capita of any city in the world—and the only big chain in town recently shut its doors.

As for Baldock, he now works for KPFA, setting up and MCing events around town, introducing the speakers as he once did at Black Oak. He still browses at Moe's, and was particularly enthusiastic about a recent find: an Italian edition of a book of photos of Fidel.

And what about those two novels, did they ever come out?

"No," he says. "Which is just fine. It's really alright. My wife asks me about this now and again, but I'm not interested. There's no way I would want them published without really working them over, and there's no way I would spend more of my life working them over. I use the other part of the brain to go in and paint, and I'm very happy about that."

11

Not Our Riot

I CALLED MY LAWYER about the 1989 anarchist riot.

"Weren't you there?" he asked.

What a question to come from your lawyer! "I may or may not have been," I said.

He laughed. "Fine. I know the feeling. It was hard to tell who was there and what was going on. It was a total mess. People were having discussions about what to do, many of them with their fists. Not only that, but there were these, basically, evil clowns who'd come from out of town and were targeting the very places we valued most—"

I interrupted, "Which businesses should have been targeted?"

Wrong question. A long speech followed about his pre-lawyer training as a carpenter and how he believes in fixing things rather than breaking them. A society has to be built rather than destroyed . . . blah blah blah. Finally, he segued into a story about trying to throw a Molotov cocktail through the old, impossibly high windows of the Telegraph B of A. The famous "Welcome to Prague" corner, if you've ever seen that photo. He scored a direct hit—the bull's-eye all Berkeley kids practice for—then waited with bated breath for the building to burst into flames a la the Isla Vista branch back in 1970. But no such luck. Damn wick must have gone out.

I thought, "Good thing I'm not getting charged by the hour for this. Or am I?"

He got to the point. "If you're looking to find out what happened on Telegraph during the riot, I can't tell you—I was with the angry mob as it went up Dwight. We crossed Telegraph, but kept going. That was when the window of Shakespeare & Co. got smashed."

The way I remember it, street people surrounded the store to protect it from any further damage, calling the anarchists phonies and telling them to go back home.

My lawyer said it might be so, he didn't know, but he never again felt welcome in Shakespeare & Co. when dropping off copies of *Slingshot*, our local anarchist rag. They'd gladly carried it in the past, but now whatever copies he left there seemed to wind up in the trash. (As the only local, visible anarchist presence, *Slingshot* was widely blamed for the riot, though nearly all the collective was against it.)

"By the way," he said, "is that store run by Marxists or Maoists or something? I've always wondered."

Dumb question—what bookstore isn't?

During the riot, the staff of Blondie's and Rasputin's were posted outside their respective stores, holding golf clubs and aluminum baseball bats to ward off would-be looters. They looked awkward and pale—a minimum-wage self-defense force much less convincing than Shakespeare & Co.'s unpaid volunteers.

But maybe I'm conflating my riots here. There were a few big ones in just a few short years.

Robert Eliason remembers being stuck inside Shakespeare & Co. during an earlier, atypical Berkeley riot, when frat boys celebrating Reagan's election took to the streets threatening to "burn down the liberal bookstores." Julian Segal was in the same store during the '91 riot when UC tried to build volleyball courts in People's Park. "That was the worst of all," he says, "worse than the '89 riots, worse than the Rodney King riots. People flipped over a police car and set it on fire. Then they closed off the street. We were holed up in the back, waiting for things to settle down."

It was during the Rodney King riot that Moe's window got smashed. Again, street people stepped in to help, this time spending the night out front to keep looters out.

Generally, though, in all the various riots the Avenue has seen over the years, the bookstores have been spared—by the rioters, at least. Pat Cody witnessed policemen intentionally breaking windows at Cody's on two different occasions. After one, a repairman arrived and took out the still-smoking tear gas canister the cops had lobbed inside. A passing patrolman saw this and ordered the tear gas returned to the scene of the crime—staying to make sure this was done and plywood nailed up so no one could remove it again. The next day, the gas was still so thick in Cody's that the staff couldn't enter. Luckily, Cody's Doubleday rep had a brother who worked for a chemical company. He suggested a product used to clean smoke-filled nightclubs, and that did the trick. The books that had absorbed the most gas sold fast—to tourists, as authentic Berkeley souvenirs.

During the bloodiest of the late-'60s riots, a first-aid station was set up in the back of Cody's to treat injuries. Fred Cody personally helped organize at least one protest march, and often served as a liaison between demonstrators and police. Any comparison between Fred and Moe is incomplete without mentioning Cody's contributions to the community, which were considerable, including his pivotal role in founding the Berkeley Free Clinic. Besides the Society for the Defense of Balding Intellectuals, Moe's only cause was the Society for the Promotion of the Water Bagel—and when it came to People's Park, he was against it from the start. Cody's took contributions for grass and shrubs, and Barb Moskowitz gave two hundred dollars for sod, but Moe himself was unconvinced. He saw the park as a false issue: a handful of people actually interested in making a park, and the rest—the great majority—only interested in creating a confrontation with the university and police. Moe felt that many of the movement's leaders were manipulative Stalinists. On both these points, he was right—and yet his right-ness blinded him from the larger truth, which is that it was still a worthy cause. Not just the park itself, but the showdown with the university and police. They had to be served notice: they couldn't just take over the city. Not without a fight.

(John Lennon struck a similarly sour note from his room at the Queen Elizabeth Hotel. "Stay at home or protest in bed," he suggested to the People's Park demonstrators—or better yet, move away. "Okay, it sounds hard to just move, migrate," he admitted, "but people have been doing it for millions of years.")

Moe stood his ground, always ready to argue good-naturedly with park activists and others who disagreed. His stance was unpopular, but his public presence and his willingness to engage and discuss kept the difference of opinion from getting too personal. Instead of closing up shop and boarding up the windows during riots, he sat at the counter in plain view with the most bored expression he could manage. As he said, "It's harder to break the window of someone you know."

The only retaliatory incident seems to have been a bit of guerrilla theater on the part of two park activists who slipped under the counter and seized the cigar box in which Moe kept the petty cash, then dashed up to the park and threw the bills into the air. Money rained down like fall leaves into the grimy hands of a tribe of happy freaks. (Shakespeare & Co.'s money was never found, safely hidden in the fiction section behind a copy of Thomas Mann's *Joseph the Provider*. A stash was discovered at Cody's—in the philosophy section behind Wittgenstein—but of drugs, not cash.)

Moe was the only business owner to defy the police-imposed nightly curfew during the original battle over the park. He thought it was important to maintain a public place where people could go (and, Barb pointed out, a rear door through which they could escape from the cops). The police responded by backing the riot control truck up against the front entrance, turning on the hose, and pumping tear gas straight into Moe's.

The cycle of violence, with the police providing their usual 90 percent, had a predictable effect on Telegraph as the 1970s dawned. Denied a real outlet for their anger, people lashed out at soft targets—mainly windows of Telegraph storefronts. Disturbed by the trend, Moe drafted a flier on the subject.

"Trashing small businesses to defend a play-ground for dealing, frisbee-throwing, and dry-fucking girls somehow lacks revolutionary stature," he wrote. "Isn't trashing more of a pseudo-revolutionary game for speed freaks—frisbees at day and rocks by night?

"While they fight for their turf, the small busi-nesses go down, replaced by larger businesses more eager to egg on the cops and better able to pay for breakage and bad seasons, followed by the exodus of street people, followed by the revival of a bigger and more plastic Telegraph."

He concluded: "Anyone who wants to argue with me or just tell me how right I am, come to a potluck at the First Baptist Church, July 15th."

Moe's dark predictions proved true, though they took longer than expected to bear fruit. The "malling" of Telegraph began in 1979 when Fraser's furniture store closed and was replaced by Miller's Outpost, a national chain. Franchises like Mrs. Field's Cookies and Waldenbooks followed, then the Gap and Crown Books—the Barnes & Noble of its time.

"It's sort of like a mugger has moved onto the block," said Bill Cartwright. "If this happened in the Grand Bazaar in a place like Tehran, the guy would be tarred and feathered. This is competition."

Moe, who had seen it coming, now shrugged it off—at least as a threat to his own business. "I'd say it was ill-advised. Whoever owns Crown made a mistake. The type of people Crown wants to attract wouldn't come to Telegraph to shop. In Walnut Creek against Books, Inc., fine. But against Cody's and me, he hasn't got it. You're not playing with some crappy bookstores here. Unless they're prepared to subsidize the store, they'll probably be out of here in a few years. They'd better stay in the shopping centers."

He was right. Crown lasted exactly three years, and no one missed it when they left. The chains turned out to be just another part of the ebb and flow in the life cycle of the Avenue (thanks partly to Barb, who vowed, "I'd never consider renting to a chain"). Waldenbooks lasted a little longer—just long enough to get set on fire for stocking *The Satanic Verses*.

Even in this regard, the chains proved second-rate. Cody's got an actual bomb, which blew a hole in the ceiling above the information desk (another pipe bomb, in the poetry section, failed to detonate).

It may have been Cody's finest moment. Salman

Rushdie, in a surprise public appearance a few months later, signed books by the remnants of the blast.

"Some authors get statues," he joked. "Others get holes."

Ugh. Hear him speak and you'll find out why a hole is what he deserved. The guy's a total ass.

12

Amoeba

KENT RANDOLPH CAME TO the Ave. in September 1979 to answer an ad in the paper: Record store manager wanted.

Randolph got to the address in time and was kept waiting two hours. Finally, a guy showed up to interview him. He had pizza sauce running down his face. His pants were down around his ass. His hair was all fucked up, and he kept running his greasy fingers through it. Of course, it was Ken—Ken Sarachan, the dreamer who never sleeps.

"Well, we need someone to do security," Ken said.

Randolph was mortified. But he'd driven all the way from Marin. Reluctantly he accepted the lesser job.

"Hold on," Ken said. "I have to fire someone."

With those fateful words, Randolph's record store career began.

Ken had second thoughts about Randolph's worth as a security guard, installing him instead at the "T-shirt Connection"—Ken's bootleg screenprinting factory. Randolph folded T-shirts as they ran off the conveyor belt. After a week, he was promoted. "Do you know how to count?" Ken asked. "Good. Inventory all the shirts."

Through a thousand similar degradations, Randolph climbed the mountain of shit—or simply outlasted the rest of Ken's staff. Within four months, he had the manager job he'd applied for. Ken needed someone to mind the daily routine at Rasputin's while he managed a half-dozen other schemes: not only Blondie's Pizza and the T-shirt Connection, but a slew of start-ups that didn't last, attempts to capitalize on the flavor of the week. There was Yogi's Yogurt, Ribs-R-Us, and a workout studio called "Some Bodies" (so says Randolph—Ken himself couldn't remember the name, and all I recall is the advertisement up in Blondie's showing two competing figures with strikingly different physiques. "I eat pizza and work out," said the one resembling Richard Simmons, and "I eat pizza and hang out," the one resembling Ken). All the businesses were on the four block stretch of Telegraph closest to campus, except Some Bodies, located further south next to the spot previously occupied by the little, family-owned pizza place which Ken had driven out of business.

Marc Weinstein was hired as Rasputin's display person in 1980. Randolph remembers the first time they met: "Marc came in to work on a display, and Ken walked in and started yelling at him, 'What the fuck are you doing?'

"And Marc, he just quit. He was really upset. He

couldn't understand why the guy was so angry and yelling at him.

"So I stopped Marc. I talked to him outside and sort of calmed him down. I said, 'Listen, whatever Ken says, you can't take it personally. That's just how he is—he wants to upset you. And if you let him upset you, he wins. You just can't listen to anything he says. You just gotta do whatever you want to do at the store. We're trying to make this a good store despite Ken.'

"Because we were into the store, you know? And at the time it was a really fun place to work. Ken would only come in a couple times a week and just raise hell and yell at people and throw things at them. I mean, I saw him throw a cash register down the stairs at a person, throw full coffee cups at people, whatever was at hand."

So Weinstein stayed on, angrily walking off the job from time to time, yet always returning. Randolph quit too, but was lured back with promises of an autonomous store in San Francisco that he could run. He fell for it—and the idea was never discussed again.

In one escape attempt Weinstein made it as far as Buffalo—his hometown—following his fantasy of opening a junkshop. "That was his dream gig," says Randolph. "Have a junkshop, hang out in the junkshop, shoot the shit, get stoned." A nice, big brick building was available for next to nothing, and his dad was willing to put up the money for the down payment—but in the end, it didn't work out. Weinstein stayed in Buffalo but went back to working for Ken, as a buyer on the Rasputin's "Record Roundups." He traveled to different towns for a week at a time—Pittsburgh, New York City, Chicago, New Orleans—where ads were placed in the local papers saying "We buy records—whole collections wanted" and the hotel or motel address where Weinstein was staying.

After a final falling out with Ken, Weinstein returned to the Bay Area, this time going to work at Streetlight Records in SF. He stayed there for several years, but all the while he was dreaming about opening his own record store, one devoted entirely to international music. From time to time, he tried to sell Randolph on the idea (the two had remained friends and also bandmates, first in new wave improv outfit the New Giraffes, then in the thirteen-piece orchestra the Beach Ogres, and finally in weird-beard band Pluto), but Randolph was unconvinced: "It sounded like a one-man operation at best."

Enter Dave Prinz, a regular Streetlight customer. A decade earlier, Prinz had owned his own business—the highly successful Captain Video chain—then sold it off while the video rental market was still red hot. Now he was rich and prematurely retired. He was a music lover, though his tastes tended to be fairly pedestrian.

He and Weinstein hit it off. The more the two men talked, the more Prinz became willing to back Weinstein's idea—and the more Weinstein's idea became tempered by Prinz's less eclectic tastes. A happy medium was found. Now all they needed was someone to do the necessary grunt work to make it happen.

Weinstein and Prinz came to visit Randolph at Rasputin's. Weinstein introduced the two and said, "You want to come hang out with us for a while?"

That was in the spring of 1990, but Randolph describes it as if it were yesterday: "We walked down the street to the corner here, and looked in at this empty space. It used to be a Mexican restaurant, but it had been closed for a while—a couple years, at least. And they kind of laid it out for me: 'We're thinking of opening up a record store. We kind of want to do it in San Francisco, but this seems to be the best location we can find. Would you be interested in helping us with that?'

"I felt kind of weird about it, because if I was going to open up a record store somewhere, I didn't want it to be near Ken. I didn't want to have any battles with him, because he doesn't play fair. And he always wins (laughs). No matter what the cost. But that's just the way it worked out."

Randolph gave notice at Rasputin's in May and started with Amoeba on June 1st—though at that time the venture was still unnamed. Randolph was renting a house on Oakland's High Street with a garage in the back, and a pool table in the garage. He boarded up the windows of the garage, secured the door, and took the felt off the pool table. The three partners spent all summer back there pricing records—a time they all remember fondly.

At first, they encouraged prospective sellers to come in person with their collections. That changed after a family from Redding arrived with an 18-foot U-Haul full of old 8-tracks. Death threats followed for weeks, variations on the "simple country folk taken advantage of by city Jews" theme. Not that house calls were without their own risks: vicious dogs and scary, coffin-collecting bikers whose records Randolph and Weinstein were scared to reject. (Moe's has its own house call story: the time Herb Bivins went out on a buy and had to be picked up miles away after being relieved of his wallet.)

Amoeba opened on November 17, 1990, and was an immediate success. Berkeley hadn't had a tolerable record store since the demise of Universal in 1983—certainly not one interested in small labels and local bands. Amoeba was everything Rasputin's wasn't, including interesting, welcoming, and cool—which is why I had to bite my tongue when Ken, on our walk, came to the subject: "Marc learned everything from me," he said.

But Randolph says he's not all wrong. The basic idea that used records make the money and the new stuff is there to bring people in—that came from Rasputin's. Some of Amoeba's pricing and organizing systems come from either Rasputin's or Streetlight. The point Ken is missing is that Weinstein, Randolph, and other employees invented those systems. Ken had no concept of what records are worth—and still doesn't, according to Randolph, inviting anyone to go to Rasputin's for proof.

The two partners and their former boss began a game of cat and mouse that continues to this day. First Ken went to Amoeba's landlord, offering to buy the building. Not to kick Amoeba out—probably—but just to mess with them, which would be more fun. Luckily the guy hated Ken, and refused his offers time and again.

Next came the Berkeley Inn site. The Berkeley Inn was a residential hotel that burned to the ground the same week Amoeba opened right across the street (Randolph was on Amoeba's roof with a hose, putting out the flying ashes that threatened to spread the blaze). The lot remained empty, first as an embattled "People's Park Annex," then as a fenced-in eyesore. When local residents and former tenants rallied for the rebuilding of the Inn, Amoeba got involved, teaming up with a nonprofit housing developer. The idea was to rebuild the low-income housing units, with a permanent home for Amoeba on the ground floor.

The plan hinged on the city dropping the outstanding taxes owed on the property. Only then would the purchase be possible.

Of course, some politicians were against it from the start. They saw the Berkeley Inn fire as an opportunity—every disaster has its opportunists—to change the lingering perception of Telegraph as a place of poverty and drugs. Foremost among them was then-Mayor Shirley Dean, who objected to the use (or loss) of public funds.

The city dragged their feet with a million hearings about the contingencies on the property, the liens on the property, the tax money owed to the city. Finally, the date passed for the sale. The deal expired.

Unlike the city, Ken wasted no time. He was on a plane the very next day with a bodyguard and a million and a half dollars in cash—in a briefcase handcuffed to his wrist. Straight to Vancouver, where he bought the Berkeley Inn site out from under Amoeba, paying the owner well over the market rate.

Checkmate!

Amoeba's owners were understandably pissed, but only for a minute. They had grown wary of the complicated zoning issues involved in partnering up with the nonprofit. They'd been committed to making it work, but after a year and a half of bullshit, they were glad just to have it resolved and admit defeat. Besides, it ended up working out better for them after all. They were able to go to plan B, enlarging the existing store instead of building a second store across the street.

Ken left the Berkeley Inn site vacant. While Amoeba expanded on their block, taking over the two neighboring storefronts (and most of the used record business in Berkeley), Ken expanded outwards—into what he calls "the Wasteland"—taking over the neighboring ten towns.

He had long ago established Rasputin's and

Blondie's satellites in Pleasant Hill. Now his outlets spread like the plague: Campbell, Newark, Vallejo, San Lorenzo—each got a little fake-Berkeley outpost, where you could get the worst trappings of Telegraph Avenue without even having to get on BART. The highly coveted jobs at these replicas went to whatever locals could be found with even more attitude than Ken's famously aggro Berkeley staff.

Ken also approached Moe's about a joint venture—a book and record store chain—but they weren't interested. Doris Moskowitz says, "Yeah, he's got a really good vision. Actually, not good, but a dark, true vision about Berkeley culture and the Wasteland— which is what he calls it, right? He says we can take the culture of Berkeley and express it differently to the Wasteland. They don't have it, they don't have culture. We've got it, let's bring it to them. I mean, there's something to that, I think that's why people come here to be part of this scene. But I couldn't see Moe's going down that road with him. We can't go there—Moe's can't go there."

Ken's altruistic mission to civilize the natives comes with the usual ulterior motive: the looting of their natural resources. Rasputin's buys up the records from the outlying areas—where Rasputin's is the only game in town—and sends them all back to Berkeley to be processed and priced. Only then are they sent, and sold, back. A miniature version of the 19th-century colonial system. Brilliant.

Yet through it all, the two Amoeba founders have

managed to retain fond feelings for Ken. "He's really smart," says Randolph, "he's really clever. For being socially retarded, he understands people pretty well—he just doesn't want to relate to them very often. You never know what Ken is going to do, which is what made working for him interesting.

"Marc and I have both stayed on good terms with him. If I see him, I'll joke around with him. In fact, last time I saw him it was at one of those dumb Berkeley meetings where nothing ever happens—you know, 'Meet Mayor Tom Bates and talk about Telegraph Avenue and its problems.' But I ended up talking to Ken, and we were kicking around ideas for what should be done up here. And I said, 'No one really plays up the Berkeley history. By People's Park, there should be a cool historical plaque, pictures and some history of the area. The Free Speech Movement, the Black Panthers, all that stuff.'

"Like three months later, Ken starts doing these window displays. Which are good, you know. I think they're okay. But he totally stole my idea."

Yet another mystery solved. Everyone up and down the Ave. had been scratching their head about why Ken—a man contemptuous of any movement besides the flow of cash—had suddenly festooned his flagship store with Panther and People's Park paraphernalia.

Now it made sense. It was another contest, another stolen recipe, another flavor of the week.

Sure enough, Ken's unveiled his newest plan for

the still-vacant Berkeley Inn site a month later: a Free Speech Museum—with luxury housing on top.

Just what Telegraph needs.

ANDY ROSS + FRED CODY

13

The Vicarious Experience

THERE'S BUT A FEW CHARACTERS left to complete the cast.

One of them is Jon Wobber.

He enters our story in the mid-'70s as a music student at Sonoma State, fifty miles north of San Francisco, where he worked at the college record library. It was cool job for a kid—mostly just sitting around listening to records to make sure they didn't skip. But there was no income during the summer months. Wobber was down to his last fifteen bucks with three weeks left before the new semester started.

The only thing he had was books—lots and lots of books. Wobber didn't know how to drive, but he did have a bike with a basket. So, he filled the basket and a backpack with titles he knew other students would like. He rode to campus, laid out his raincoat on the grass, and spread the books on top.

"That was the beginning of my career as a book-seller," he says now, chuckling a bit. "You learn to sell books quick when you've got to carry them on your back."

As bookselling overtook his library job, Wobber

rode all over Sonoma County looking for more stock. When his destination was too far to reach by bike, he stuck out his thumb. Then one day he got the ride that changed his life. No sooner had he settled into his seat and some casual conversation, Wobber realized just who it was he was riding with. "You're the famous Harvey Segal!" he beamed.

If the name doesn't ring a bell, don't worry. Every town and time has its celebrities, big and small. Some make it in the tabloids and some, like Segal, the front page of the local paper. Segal was famous in the mid-'70s, in towns like Petaluma and Cotati, as the much-loved professor locked in a heated battle with the Sonoma State University administration over tenure. They had denied it, he had demanded it, and moved heaven and earth (and much of the student body) to overturn their decision. It was the kind of fight everyone likes: pleasantly simple in its dimensions and nicely polarizing—no agonizing soul-searching necessary to choose sides. Best of all, it was one struggle that might actually be possible to win—which Segal eventually did, though that victory was yet to come at the time of Wobber's ride.

Coincidentally, both Wobber and Segal were headed to the same place, and with the same purpose. Segal, it turned out, was not just a beleaguered sociology professor—he was also an old hand at the book business, having started at the tender age of twelve rooting through the shelves of New York's Book Row for stuff to buy and resell. Nowadays he searched mostly just to round out his own library, though on trips like this—to the Sebastopol flea market—he was unlikely to find the Mayan and Aztec history texts he loved. Instead he found art books and literary gems which he bought mostly just out of habit, exchanging them later for cash or credit.

Following that fateful trip, Wobber returned to the lawn at Sonoma State, and Segal to teaching (with tenure) and scouting on the side. But there was yet another passenger along for the ride, listening in to the conversation as Wobber and Segal warmed to each other—a book scout even younger than Segal in his days on New York's Fourth Avenue: Julian, Segal's eight-year-old son.

As it happens, I know Julian, so I invited him to tell his side of the story, hoping to uncover some scandalous details the adults had left out. Sadly, his version corresponded almost word for word with what Wobber had said, the only difference being a nostalgia Julian feels for the mid-'70s in Sonoma County—a scene he witnessed but was too young to join: the free-for-all environment, the couples fucking on the lawn. "I would've liked to have been eighteen back then," Julian sighed.

Who among us hasn't wondered if they might have gotten more action if only they were born a little earlier or later? But we're slaves to time and circumstance—in this case two repressed guys in the back of a cafe (Au Coquelet—which we once derided as "No Coke, No Lay") talking about the world of our fathers.

According to Julian, Segal won the hard-fought

battle for tenure but got fed up with teaching just a few years later. He and his wife—Julian's mom—left Sonoma and relocated to the Bay Area, where they split up. Segal knew both Moe and Cartwright from his long years as a book scout. He'd walked into Moe's original store right after arriving in California from New York. Cartwright he described as having a mellow disposition and a penchant for studying French (apparently a different Cartwright from the one everyone else met—but then, we show different sides of ourselves to different friends).

Now Cartwright offered Segal a job at Shakespeare & Co., and Segal accepted.

At the same time, Segal became an active member of the First Unitarian Church in Kensington (called the "First Unitarian Church of Berkeley" to avoid unpleasant acronyms). There he heard tell of a Unitarian woman named Jackie Miskel who was planning to open a bookstore in Walnut Creek. Ever the scout, Segal drove out to sell her some books—and ended up with something else.

("Yeah, pretty funny," says Julian. In fact, he and I also met through the Unitarian church. He was in the youth group and I was in a band that played every shitty, ridiculous show we could find, the kind I'd now go to any lengths to avoid.)

Wobber had by then established his own shop in Cotati, "the Vicarious Experience." It was the only bookstore in town, taking over for the recently closed Eeyore Books.

But, let's put the Vicarious Experience on the back burner for now—along with the simmering Segal/Miskel romance—while we focus on another North County character, Eeyore Books' former owner, who'd shuttered his shop and moved to Berkeley in order to answer the question, "What's the difference between a schlemiel and a schlemazel?"

Ladies and gentlemen, may I introduce: Andy Ross.

Ross was no WWII pilot, not a writer for *The Economist*, nor the kind of person who draws everyone's attention when he enters the room. He was a small-town hippie still wet behind the ears, of short stature and just thirty years old when he came to Berkeley to buy Cody's Books from its founders and owners, Fred and Pat.

Admittedly, theirs were hard shoes to fill, but Ross never came close. One former employee recalls Ross as a "difficult, combative, short-tempered schlub." In fact, no one I spoke to described him without lapsing into Yiddish, a language not known for its tender endearments. Ross was held beneath contempt rather than hated, which at least confers a certain kind of respect. Even decades later, he's still trying to defend himself and measure up. "For twenty years, I was referred to as the new owner of Cody's," he wrote in 2006. "I think I have finally outgrown that moniker."

Responses to that ranged from "Fat chance!" to "It'll follow him to the grave."

Ross ended up owning Cody's Books even longer

than Fred and Pat had, yet he remained a nobody rather than becoming a legend, partly because he hid behind their name and legacy to pursue his own agenda.

"I've tried to keep the values Fred Cody had for this store," Ross said when unveiling plans for a 15,000 square foot addition to the building, citing the need for more display space. When construction was complete in 1986 in time for Cody's thirty-year anniversary, the new set-up included a gallery, party room, and a 100-seat "Parisian-style" sidewalk cafe. "I want it to be a little more upscale," said Ross when asked how "Cody's Cafe" would compare to the Med.

Only a fourth of the new space was used for books—and when Ross's upscale cafe closed in just two years, the Med looked on Sphinx-like, smiling to itself.

"I would rather have one great store in one great location than two—or two hundred—mediocre ones," Ross proclaimed, then opened a Cody's on Fourth Street, a shopping enclave best described by the old '60s adage "three parts bullshit and one part boredom," followed by another near Union Square aimed at the gift book and greeting card crowd.

And all the while, he was mouthing off to the media about the terrible evil of the chain stores. The chains, the chains, the chains. They were coming to get him. They were ruining his business—all three of them.

As for his relationship with Telegraph, it was thorny at best. His support for anti-homeless legislation earned him many enemies on the street—and angry graffiti that included swastikas drawn in chalk.

Ross's response (a rally against anti-semitism with soundbites like "there's a limit to free speech!") was ridiculous. The media frenzy that followed was worse, painting the homeless and their allies as anti-semites.

The truth is, no one knew Ross was a Jew. Misguided or not, the swastikas were meant as political commentary, and to play the persecution card seemed cheap and in bad taste.

Even other business owners found him unbearable—and the feeling was mutual. When asked to comment on his next-door neighbor Moe, Ross struggled to find something nice to say, but failed.

"Well, he usually has a tuna fish sub for lunch," Ross finally offered.

DON SCHENKER + MOE
ON MOE'S 70TH BIRTHDAY

14

The Hitchhiker Takes the Wheel

ROSS WAS BUT THE FIRST of a new generation on the block. Fred Cody had died not long after selling Ross the shop. Then Reprint Mint was sold to a new owner in 1985, and Don Schenker died soon after. Sam Bercholz still owned Shambhala, but hadn't been there in years, having relocated to Boston (after quickly tiring of Boulder—go figure) where Shambhala Publishing continued to thrive. He even attempted a new bookstore there, but the experiment didn't last. Longtime employee Philip Barry was left in charge of the Berkeley Shambhala and became its public face. A customer-turned-clerk, Barry had worked his way up to manager and part owner. It was only a matter of time before Bercholz gave up his stake.

One by one, the old regime was being replaced. Only Moe and Cartwright remained.

Meanwhile in Walnut Creek, Miskel was kicking ass. She'd started from scratch with no prior book experience, and just learned along the way. Her store, Bonanza Books, was a breakaway success. Previous to that, the only thing close to a used bookstore in the area was a crappy strip-mall paperback exchange.

Now, following Miskel's good fortune, a stampede of other bookstores and cafes came over the hill. Soon every local paper had a feature piece about "the new Berkeley: Walnut Creek," where you could escape homeless people, minorities, crime, and culture—and finally enjoy a good book and a latte in peace.

Thankfully, Bonanza survived the competition as well as the comparison.

Miskel and Segal were still a hot item. Hot, hot, hot. But they kept to their separate stores, Miskel in the suburbs and Segal in the wilds of Shakespeare & Co., where he was adjusting to a new life on the wrong side of the counter.

Then, one day in 1988, Cartwright approached Segal with a proposition. Nearly twenty-five years had passed since the broken promise that had created Shakespeare & Co., and still there was no ice cream and no reconciliation with Moe. Cartwright was tired. He wanted to get out of the store and onto the tennis court.

Imagine sitting all day on that corner of Telegraph—a fairly intense corner, through which some of the worst people on earth pass—and right across the street is someone who hates your guts, maybe staring out the window as we speak.

Good. Now imagine doing it again—and again, and again—eight thousand times. No wonder he was tired. It was a fate worse than death—though death, it turned out, was also part of the fate. Cartwright was seized by a fatal heart attack on the tennis courts he'd been waiting so long to hit, shortly after selling Segal and Miskel the shop.

Co-owners now of Shakespeare & Co., Segal and Miskel wisely decided not to combine their two stores. Some of Shakespeare & Co.'s golf and gardening books could be sent out to the suburbs—little things like that—but in terms of management and bookkeeping, the two businesses were separated even as their owners tied the knot. The only thing mutual was support.

The same manager was kept on staff: Tim Hildebrandt, who now owns Spectator Books on Piedmont. Segal made a few changes (fewer new books, more remainders, a pickier selection) but otherwise continued to run the store much as Cartwright had. Whether or not Moe's old grudge carried over to Shakespeare & Co.'s new owners is a matter of debate. Segal's son Julian says absolutely not. Everyone else says yes—though certainly it was a lesser grudge, perhaps one extended to all bookstore owners alike.

"There was never anything positive said," remembers Moe's daughter Doris. "Moe thought that Moe's was the way a bookstore should be. He didn't have much time for the way other people run bookstores. He could be pretty judgmental."

In my conversations with Doris, that judgmental attitude is something that came up repeatedly, both as a personal quality of Moe's and as an attitude that became ingrained in the character of the store—one she has tried to discourage since taking ownership (though changing some of the lifers on staff, she admits, may be a lost cause).

It is true that nowadays when a guy walks in with stuff to sell, no one loudly yells, "We don't buy stolen books!" causing every customer in the place to turn and stare and the poor schmuck to flush, half in embarrassment and half in anger.

Of course, that schmuck was me—or, rather, I was among countless schmucks who got that same kind of treatment every time they came in—and it wasn't something that endeared me to Moe's or Moe himself, sitting there like a judge. I agree with Doris about how annoying it was.

And yet walking into the modern, kinder, gentler Moe's, where a new, California-born generation has taken charge, one experiences a sense of loss. The New York-style verbal sparring is not the only thing gone.

By the time you're ready to take on your elders as equals, they're dead. That's the deal. I get it. But every time I enter Moe's, I wonder why it took so long to ready ourselves. Was I—and the rest of my generation—coddled and slow, or were Moe and the rest of the "colorful characters" so patronizing and so generous with their judgment that they never gave us room to grow? That's the question.

Sam Spenger, longtime Shakespeare & Co. employee (and cousin to the famous Berkeley fishmonger family) remembers feeling like a little kid every time he dealt with Moe, even well into his thirties. "How you like working for Harvey?" Moe would say, blowing cigar smoke in Spenger's face. "It was scary," Spenger says. "But in a good way."

Then again, how did Moe feel? That was the era of his divorce from Barb and the beginning of his decline. Deserted by most of his lieutenants, surrounded by a bunch of kids, Moe sat around telling the same stale jokes and blowing the same stale smoke. And Telegraph, is it really the place to look out the window on a day when everyone else is dead—both friends and enemies—and expect to see hope? Frankly, no— though someone else was surely walking down the street at that moment for the very first time, seeing it all wide-eyed.

Moe did come to find a new lease on life: a fellow Bronx native named Renee Liebermann, who wrote short stories under the pseudonym Renee Blitz (look for her upcoming collection *Shiksa Pussy* on Regent Press). Liebermann became Moe's second wife. He quit smoking and cut back to working only five days a week. But it was too little, too late.

Doris had started working at the store after graduating from Mills College in 1990. Julian, Segal's son, began at Shakespeare & Co. in 1988. They were literally the new generation, bookstore kids who'd grown up in the business, yet they were not looked upon as heirs apparent to their fathers' empires. Doris was fired not once but twice ("Moe didn't believe in nepotism," she insists). Her two half-sisters from Barb's first marriage also came to work at the store, and were both summarily dismissed. Doris, however, showed her resolve as well as her affinity for the family business, and was rehired. (As for her half-sisters, one now works for the University of Auckland in New Zealand, the other as a real estate agent in Modesto.)

Julian's attempts to escape his father's store were also short-lived. Truly a bookish kid, he'd worked at three Bay Area bookstores even before his dad landed the job at Shakespeare & Co. Julian's next fifteen years were spent working there, with breaks for each time he tried to leave the nest. First it was Portland, working at Powell's. Next, Ursus Books in New York, then Logos in Santa Cruz (another Moe's spin-off—owner John Livingston started out in Moe's record department in the mid-'60s). Finally, New York again, at the lovely though oft-overlooked Skyline Books.

But Julian's luck with moving was lousy. Layoffs, the rain, terrorist attacks—it was always something that kept him coming back.

And the last member of Telegraph's new regime? None other than Jon Wobber, the Sonoma State bookseller last seen proudly cutting the ribbon on his own shop. Wobber's friendship with Segal had endured since their first chance meeting. Now Wobber became Shakespeare & Co.'s North Bay scout, bringing books down to Berkeley to sell, just as Segal had done in the Cartwright days.

Yes, the hitchhiker had learned to drive.

Wobber's shop, the Vicarious Experience, was not exactly a thriving business. With an average take of thirty-five bucks a day, it was a living, but not by much. At the same time, Segal was short-staffed, so an arrangement was made: Wobber could keep his own store open on weekends and drive down to work at Shakespeare & Co. during the week.

Andy Ross didn't even recognize his old Cotati neighbor and competitor when Wobber first showed up on the block. But then, a whole decade had passed.

Julian seriously considered buying Shakespeare & Co. when his dad and Miskel retired in 2004 (also selling off Bonanza and another bookstore Miskel had started in Clayton). Julian had no doubts about his own book knowledge, but was less sure about his business skills. Without a Miskel of his own to share the burden and the rewards with, he finally decided to pass.

Instead, Wobber bought the place, and there you'll find him today, looking a little browbeaten but with a mischievous twinkle in his eye. He closed the Vicarious Experience but still keeps a home in Cotati, commuting back and forth.

Stan Spenger, former head buyer at Shakespeare & Co., is now at Pegasus. "And then I came down to my little slice of heaven," he says.

Segal comes into Pegasus from time to time with a fresh stack of books he's scouted, preferring to bring them to Spenger, the former employee he remembers fondly, rather than return to the store he once owned.

Segal's son Julian now works in publishing, but warns me not to bother looking for books at the thrift store next door to his office—he checks it three times a week, reselling the best stuff to Wobber.

Aye, what a mess. What a tangled web. But what about Moe?

He died in 1997—and when he did, no one took it seriously. It was April Fool's Day.

Moe died? And then what?

Then nothing—that's the point. You become the punch line of your own joke.

ACE BACKWORDS

15

The Last Word

I WALK DOWN TELEGRAPH, saying my farewells.

Chanukah is long over, New Year's too, and the winter has passed. Time now to pack up my notes and interview tapes and head back east.

One last chance to check my PO box before I leave, one last chance to hear any late-breaking news. It's also my last chance to see Telegraph in the present, after months steeped in stories of how it used to be, how it came to be, what it might have been.

Yet the present is elusive, as hard to find as Sam Hardin, the third Rambam partner and this story's missing link. Following a lead that he was still alive and living in South Berkeley, I finally managed to track him down just the day before it was time to go—but it turned out I was already too late. Alzheimer's had found Hardin a year ahead of me. Now he doesn't remember a thing.

At this point, I may know more about Rambam than anyone alive. That's what happens: you come upon something as a curious, enthusiastic outsider and soon find yourself the resident expert. Now Doris even calls with questions about the store her dad co-owned.

Telegraph is the same way. Someone else should have written the social history of the Avenue disguised as an argument between two unreasonable men. Someone born earlier, someone who stayed later rather than leaving the first chance they could get. And yet, it was I who couldn't get away from it in the end.

Now Cody's is boarded up and dark. Out front sits Ace Backwords with a long line of card tables neatly stacked with books. He sells them all—from precious art folios to old fanzines—for a quarter each. Long ago, Ace had a fanzine of his own, then went on to draw comics, publish a calendar of Telegraph street people, and author a book, *Surviving on the Streets*. Presently he appears comatose, with a far-off stare. I stand directly in front, flagging him down, trying to get his attention in order to say hi for the first time in twenty years. Finally he sees me and takes off the headphones.

"How've you been?" I ask.

"Bad," he admits. "I've been feeling nostalgic for the early '80s. The mid-'90s were actually pretty great, too—but I've been in a downward spiral for the last ten years."

His casualness and candor make me inexplicably happy: the idea that a person can have not just a bad day, but a bad decade, and still wake up curious to see what the next one will bring. Also, I happen to disagree about his trajectory, which I've followed out of the corner of my eye, in passing, over time. Though I enjoyed some of Ace's old work, his fairly new role as Avenue bookseller seems to me to be the pinnacle of his career. Not only is it a bold makeover for Ace, it provides a much-needed service for the rest of us. Not since Ken Sarachan's earliest days has anyone regularly sidewalk-sold used books here.

Ace clearly relishes the compliment, but coyly deflects it. "Somehow I didn't picture myself at fifty selling junk on the street corner," he says. "But I do sell some great books—it's amazing what kind of stuff you can find."

Pointing at the shuttered Cody's building, I rib him a little: "In one of your calendars, you called this 'the intellectual center of Berkeley.'"

"I did?" He seems genuinely surprised. "Well, I must have been lying. It's the center of nothing now. Center of skid row, I guess."

Indeed, the scene is bleak. Ever since Andy Ross closed the Telegraph Cody's in 2006, the building has remained vacant. Berkeley's intellectual center may have been half a block south, but Cody's was still a crucial part of the Avenue's ecosystem, one that is sorely missed. Ross's farewell speech to the Ave. is still taped inside the window. "Americans have come to value uniformity and predictability over diversity," he said, taking a superior, admonishing tone as usual, while furthering the process he claimed to hate. Cody's two other locations were kept open: Fourth Street and Union Square—two of the most homogenous, predictable areas of the Bay.

And while Ross complained, conservatives in the city government did what they do best: punish and blame. The poor, the homeless, and the Left were all scapegoated for creating an "anti-business atmosphere." The usual specious claims of high crime were heard, the perennial cries for an increase in police, though in fact crime rates on the Ave. have been mostly steady or in decline for the past thirty years (check the statistics—I did!).

Standing on that corner now, I remember a veteran Cody's employee who gloated when the Berkeley Inn across the street was razed: "My view will be greatly improved," he said. "Now I'll be able to see the Berkeley Hills."

And how about that view? One notices in it anything but the rolling hills. Instead, two decades have passed—both Ace's longed-for mid-'90s and his ten-year downward spiral—and an ugly, empty lot still remains where the Inn once stood. That makes two eyesores at one intersection, and I'm not talking about Ace and me.

At the present rate, it may soon be three. Amoeba's SF and LA outlets are hugely successful, but the original Telegraph store is barely breaking even. The question, "How long can it last?" is on everyone's lips. (Up the street, Rasputin's is in much the same boat: treading water in Berkeley while expanding elsewhere, most recently into former Tower locations in Mountain View, Stockton, and Fresno. Ken Sarachan, however, has nothing to fear, since he owns the property his stores are on—and oh, so much more. The big news where Ken is concerned is that after thirty-five years, he's back to where he started, paying a dollar a box for used paperbacks. Part of the new Mountain View Rasputin's is Rasputin's Books.)

Luckily, the fourth corner of Telegraph and Haste houses Mario's La Fiesta, a Mexican restaurant that shows no sign of instability. Mario's has been around longer even than Moe's, and Mario and his wife Rosalinda (who live in the warehouse squeezed between Amoeba and People's Park) can still be seen every day strolling down the Avenue holding hands.

As they pass, I sigh. Julia Stalingrad, "the Bubble Lady," limps along behind, looking none too bubbly. It's one of those days—or maybe just the place. Students keep getting in her way. This season is the worst, with legions of freshmen blocking the sidewalks, sheepishly waiting for the light to change. ("These students could care less about free speech," Baldock griped. "They would probably oppose it.") None, of course, stop to glance at the books on Ace's table, leaving us to gossip without interruption.

The latest item is about the reappearance of Peggy Rita, the old Print Mint co-owner, now sole owner since her husband Bob's death. Following a break-in at Print Mint's old Folger Street warehouse, Rita recently arrived at the Book Zoo—a wonderful store further down the Avenue—with two police officers in tow, wrongly accusing the owners of selling stolen goods. That's what it takes in Berkeley to get a Baby Boomer to visit your business: a panic to recover "priceless" '60s relics that have been sitting for years gathering dust. Had she shown up on her own and actually bought a book, it would've been headline news. (The story of Book Zoo and Books Not Com—both with owners who worked at Moe's but were fired because of old fears about employees gathering stock for their own stores—will have to wait for volume two.)

The other hot gossip is the complete demise of Cody's. Shortly after vacating the Telegraph store, Ross sold the remaining two Cody's to a Japanese corporation, Yohan Inc., owner of eighteen bookstores in Japan plus publishing interests in the States. Yup, he sold out to the chains, the very first one willing to buy him out, and they closed the Union Square store and then Fourth Street too, opening a new Cody's downtown in 2008. (Strangely, no one complained about all the nasty yuppies loitering on Fourth Street, driving business away.) The new place was a void, less than zero: a foreign-owned airport-style bookstore with a sign outside that said "Shopping locally helps Berkeley."

What a fucking joke!

Now, after just three months, it's closed too.

Ace surprises me with some sympathy for—of all people—Andy Ross, whose antagonism towards the homeless community is legendary. "I'm antagonistic towards it too," Ace laughs, "even though I'm part of it." As for the other bookstores, he says the Shakespeare & Co. staff has been most amiable, buying books from him as well as bringing donations. The guys from Moe's seem grumpy—they don't even stop to look.

And now, time draws to a close. I bid farewell to Ace, to Cody's, to Amoeba, to Mario's La Fiesta, and the

Avenue's open wound that was once the Berkeley Inn. In a sort of reverse homesickness (surely the Germans have a word for it) I walk towards Dwight Way, where I've locked up my bike. I pass Moe's, now managed by the stoic Gene "Gino" Barone and owned by Doris Moskowitz, who, along with her husband Johnny, also runs a toy store on College Avenue called "Boss Robot Hobby." I raise my finger to Lhasa Karnak, which took over the old Shambhala storefront when they closed in 2003. (Shambhala owner Philip Barry briefly went on to work for both Cody's and Moe's before taking a job at a Reno bookstore in order to be closer to his son. Fagan is now a Boston-based rare book dealer, specializing in art books from the former Austro-Hungarian Empire. Bercholz has "simplified his life" and left the publishing house in the hands of his daughter Sarah.)

Finally, I pass Reprint Mint and Shakespeare & Co., "Red Rockets" graffiti still etched into the cement outside. As I fumble with my lock, a panhandler begins his familiar refrain, "Excuse me, could you spare some—"

And then he stops, mid-sentence.

"Oh, it's you," he says, fondly. "I haven't seen you in a long time."

He looks me over from head to toe like a rarely seen relative. "Man," he sighs. "I watched you grow up!"

I look at him with only the vaguest recollection, but the same familiar feeling I get from these businesses, these streets, these trees. I barely know this guy—but have been passing him my entire life.

While my eyes mist up, his look preoccupied. Perhaps he's said too much. More likely he's doing the math, counting the years, thinking, "If he's grown up, then I've grown something else."

We look at each other in shock at the accidental intimacy of the interchange. And then, with a smile and a wave, I ride away.

My thoughts turn to Moe, the man who, more than anyone, made Telegraph what it is today.

"I like this street," he said. "Even though it makes me sad."

About the Author

Aaron Cometbus has written seven novels and published the fanzine *Cometbus* since 1981.

ABOUT PM PRESS

PM Press is an independent, radical publisher of critically necessary books for our tumultuous times. Our aim is to deliver bold political ideas and vital stories to all walks of life and arm the dreamers to demand the impossible. Founded in 2007  by a small group of people with decades of publishing, media, and organizing experience, we have sold millions of copies of our books, most often one at a time, face to face. We're old enough to know what we're doing and young enough to know what's at stake. Join us to create a better world.

PM Press
PO Box 23912
Oakland, CA 94623
www.pmpress.org

PM Press in Europe
europe@pmpress.org
www.pmpress.org.uk

FRIENDS OF PM PRESS

These are indisputably momentous times—the financial system is melting down globally and the Empire is stumbling. Now more than ever there is a vital need for radical ideas.

In the many years since its founding—and on a mere shoestring—PM Press has risen to the formidable challenge of publishing and distributing knowledge and entertainment for the struggles ahead. With hundreds of releases to date, we have published an impressive and stimulating array of literature, art, music, politics, and culture. Using every available medium, we've succeeded in connecting those hungry for ideas and information to those putting them into practice.

Friends of PM allows you to directly help impact, amplify, and revitalize the discourse and actions of radical writers, filmmakers, and artists. It provides us with a stable foundation from which we can build upon our early successes and provides a much-needed subsidy for the materials that can't necessarily pay their own way. You can help make that happen—and receive every new title automatically delivered to your door once a month—by joining as a Friend of PM Press. And, we'll throw in a free T-shirt when you sign up.

Here are your options:
- **$30 a month** Get all books and pamphlets plus a 50% discount on all webstore purchases
- **$40 a month** Get all PM Press releases (including CDs and DVDs) plus a 50% discount on all webstore purchases
- **$100 a month** Superstar—Everything plus PM merchandise, free downloads, and a 50% discount on all webstore purchases

For those who can't afford $30 or more a month, we have **Sustainer Rates** at $15, $10 and $5. Sustainers get a free PM Press T-shirt and a 50% discount on all purchases from our website.

Your Visa or Mastercard will be billed once a month, until you tell us to stop. Or until our efforts succeed in bringing the revolution around. Or the financial meltdown of Capital makes plastic redundant. Whichever comes first.